Grace for (

CW01646867

UK Englisl

Part I

Alpha: Harnessing Grace

Part II

Omega: The Way of Truth

Published 2025

Edition 1.1

ISBN: 978-1-9162485-2-6

With special thanks to

Sarah, Charlotte, Lucy,

Capt. David, Kim, Mike, Pauline, Tildy, Franz

Inspiration: Taylor & Tyler, Hank & John, The Paul Bro's & Co's, the WR Team, General Conference

Cover design © Franz Sidney

Hebrew & Greek references: biblehub.com, Strong's Exhaustive Concordance

References

The King James Version of the Bible (KJV) has been used for most references, as it is the most commonly owned English Bible in homes today and my preferred formal equivalent. However, the English Standard Version (ESV) is also highly recommended. I would avoid a dynamic equivalence (thought-for-thought) version (such as the NLT), but that is certainly up to you. It won't take long to wrap your head around the formal language of the KJV. This book references original Hebrew and Greek using the interlinear on biblehub.com. In-line scripture references and quotes are provided instead of footnotes, making the words of scripture more accessible for readers. Some passages have been shortened to focus on the topic, so readers are encouraged to read the surrounding verses to gain a fuller context.

Scripture references will be formatted as follows: [Revelation 19:7-9; 21:1-4]. The book and chapter are listed first, e.g., Revelation Chapter 19, followed by the verses after the colon: 7 to 9. If another book is referenced, it will follow a semicolon; if the reference continues within the same book, another chapter and verse are listed without repeating the book name. For example, 21:1–4 still refers to the Book of Revelation.

When a Greek or Hebrew word is referenced, the corresponding Strong's Concordance number is usually given in brackets. These numbers, such as the Strong's reference for grace, *Charis* (5485), were assigned by James Strong and his team in the late nineteenth century.

They help to clarify original meaning within scripture text, providing a deeper understanding for the reader.

All references to the Holy Ghost, Holy Spirit, and Spirit are used interchangeably. Any underlined or **bold** text in *scripture quotes* is the author's own emphasis. Any inclination toward Hypostatic Union or Nestorianism within this book is purely incidental and not intended. The author's view will become apparent by the end of the supplements in Part I.

The author has drawn from many resources over the years and is writing of his own accord, not at the behest of any organisation. All views expressed are from the author's perspective. Readers are kindly asked to look past any imperfect prose to see the light of the Lord between the lines.

Two Parts

Jesus Christ is the Alpha and Omega [Revelation 1:8]. We hear much about the Alpha principles but less about the Omega. To Nicodemus, at the beginning of his ministry, Jesus said we must be born-again to enter the kingdom of heaven, but to his disciples at the end, the Lord said we must have oil in our lamps, feed the hungry, clothe the naked etc. While we embrace the Alpha principles, we also embrace the Omega when we say we believe in him.

Alpha: Harnessing Grace (Part I)

In Christian history, there has been tension between two schools of thought: salvation by grace and salvation by works. After thirty years of discussions with various Christians, I can confidently say that a misunderstanding has occurred, creating an apparent chasm between these beliefs. In reality, it is not one or the other. It is not a choice one has to make.

Simply put, most people who speak of being saved by grace agree that one cannot be truly saved if they continue in sin. One must be transformed by grace, or they were never truly saved in the first place. A clear example is someone who claims to be saved but continues to commit adultery with his neighbour's wife. Such a person will not be sitting in heaven with Jesus, laughing that he got away with it. There is always a measure of change expected in the character of a new and growing Christian. When Jesus was confronted with the woman caught in adultery, he told her to 'Go, and sin no more,' not 'Carry on; I've got your sins covered.' Every Christian I have sincerely spoken with about grace has expressed this view of turning from sin, also known as repentance.

The same principle applies to those who emphasize works. A person who strives to keep the commandments and fails daily would not claim they are trying to save themselves through their good works. Almost all who seek to follow Jesus testify that their good works would be in vain without his atoning sacrifice. No matter how well we love our neighbour, we are all lost and fallen without the Redeemer. If we could get ourselves to heaven without Jesus, there would have been no point in his great and last sacrifice for us.

Jesus loves unity, while the devil loves division. Part I of this book seeks to explore Jesus' teachings on this issue and identify where potential derailments of unity have occurred. In Jesus' day the temple had a dividing wall separating the Jews from the Gentiles, ensuring no unclean person entered the area. By understanding the doctrine of Christ, we can eliminate the dividing walls between us, just as he did with the Jews and Gentiles in the past.

'*For he is our peace, who hath made both one, and hath broken down the middle wall of partition between us*' [Ephesians 2:14]

Omega: The Way of Truth (Part II)

Christians love to sing and dance, praising the Lord and giving glory to his name. We also love to let our light shine by serving others, thereby fulfilling the two great commandments to love God and love our neighbours.

When we serve, we may be doing good work, but God is less interested in what we do and more concerned with who we are becoming. When we exercise our muscles in the gym of service, we grow spiritually stronger and become more fit for the kingdom. It doesn't matter where we develop our benevolent biceps or diligent deltoids; what matters is that we are gradually transforming into the image of Christ, becoming one with him and loving others as he loves them.

Jesus showed us the way home, clearing the thorns and thistles to help us get there [Genesis 3:18]. Now, he expects us to learn the rules of his house as a token gesture in return so we can feel comfortable at his table.

He said, '*Be ye therefore perfect*', which means *finished* or *complete*. 'Omega: The Way of Truth' explores ten specific ways scripture encourages us to become a finished product, reaching the fulfilment of our intended creation. While we celebrate the new beginning Jesus offers us, we pick up both ends of the stick of Judah, understanding that Jesus taught us 'the way back' to the tree of life, not 'the way out.'

'*that the man of God may be complete [perfect], equipped for every good work.*' [2 Timothy 3:17 ESV]

Where We Started

The Gospel of John is known for its high Christology, meaning it focuses on Jesus' divinity more than the narrative of his life found in the other three synoptic gospels. I love John for his meticulous recording of events surrounding the Last Supper.

The world's most famous Christian scripture is John 3:16, but the title of this book is taken from a couple of chapters earlier in John 1:16.

'*And of his fulness have all we received, and grace for grace.*' KJV

Another angle on this same verse is taken when we study the ESV,

'*For from his fullness we have all received, grace in place of grace*' [including the ESV footnote].

The Greek manuscripts from which these English words are translated show that the fullness of God's grace is given to us in exchange for, or as a substitute for the grace we show others. It is therefore fair to render the passage into English as follows,

'*For of his fullness, we have all received, indeed, grace in exchange for grace.*'

I particularly like the inclusion of another footnote by the writers of the ESV (referring to Matthew 25:29), which implies that those who use their [grace] will be given more [grace], while those who do not use [grace] will have their gift removed. Thus, we see that more grace is received when grace is doubled, or mirrored, by us. The concept that Jesus gives more grace to those who have it and takes away grace from those who do not is central to understanding his teachings on forgiveness [Matthew 18], the mysteries [Matthew 13], and receiving the talents or attributes of Christ [Matthew 25].

Indeed, Jesus taught that he is willing to give us the right to rule and reign with him in the kingdom of Heaven if we show love one to another, in the same way he has shown love to us. This book aims to teach the doctrine of grace gradually from the viewpoint of Jesus, John, Peter, James, Jude, and Paul instead of just focusing on a few of Paul's words alone. We will use Sola Whola rather than Sola Paula.

If you are finding the above snapshot of the book at odds with your current viewpoint, please take the time to read Part I and Part II, then return to this opening page and see if T. S. Eliot's famous quote has been realised,

We shall not cease from exploration
And the end of all our exploring
Will be to arrive where we started
And know the place for the first time.

My object in writing this book has been to bring unity to the Christian world, that we might have grace for each other, as Jesus taught [See Ephesians 4:7].

Introduction

In the Garden of Eden, the Devil tempted Eve to eat from the Tree of Knowledge of good and evil by quoting her the scripture about being free to eat any fruit she wanted. As lifted from the Hebrew, with commas added to separate the sentence construction, the Lord God said to Adam,

'*of every, tree, of the garden, freely, you may eat*' [Genesis 2:16]

which does sound like Yoda from Star Wars speaking back-to-front, but that is the rhythm of Hebrew. As stated, this free blessing from God was correctly quoted by Lucifer to Eve as follows,

'*Indeed, has said, God, not, you shall eat, of every, tree, of the garden?*' [Genesis 3:1]

Satan correctly quoted God, but deliberately forgot to include the commandment which the Lord gave next,

'*but of the tree, of the knowledge, of good, and evil, not, you shall eat*' [Genesis 2:17]

Lucifer omitted the strict commandment of the Lord not to eat the fruit of the tree of knowledge, and just gave the general free blessing, in the hope of deceiving Eve.

Similarly, there is a problem in the world that Satan is happy for us to quote the free blessings of scripture but would rather have us ignore the commandments. If Satan told straight lies, nobody would believe him, so he has to use half-truths.

One lesson we can take away is that using single scriptural verses to base our hope for salvation is fraught with difficulty.

When Paul said,

'*if thou shalt confess with thy mouth the Lord Jesus, and shalt believe in thine heart that God hath raised him from the dead, thou shalt be saved.*' [Romans 10:9]

he was essentially referencing John,

'*For God so loved the world, that he gave his only begotten Son, that whosoever believeth in him should not perish, but have everlasting life.*' [John 3:16]

This concept is true and forms the hope of our salvation in Jesus, but taken on its own, it sounds like all we have to do to receive eternal life is say a prayer something like,

'Jesus, I believe you are the Son of God and have been raised from the dead; please save me now.'

Both scriptures in John and Romans make no mention of repentance, but most churches accept we have to add that in because it was a core message during Jesus' ministry on earth. So we end up with a prayer something like the 'sinner's prayer' found on Wikipedia,

'Dear Lord Jesus, I know that I am a sinner, and I ask for Your forgiveness. I believe You died for my sins and rose from the dead. **I turn from my sins** and invite You to come into my heart and life. I want to trust and follow You as my Lord and Saviour.'

This prayer admits at the core that one must do more than say 'I believe'. It states that we will **turn from our sins** through repentance and follow Jesus in the way he walked. Anything less than embarking on this journey is like believing in a miracle cure for cancer but refusing to follow the doctor's directions. Single scripture verses need context added so we are not tempted to ignore the rest of Jesus' commandments, as Lucifer tried with Eve. I am grateful that the 'Sinner's Prayer' builds into it the need to repent and then actively follow Jesus.

We are justified (forgiven) by God's grace when we repent [Romans 3:24] but sanctified through grace and truth [John 17:17-19], which is his strength and his word.

'*For the law [of works] was given by Moses, but grace and truth came by Jesus Christ.*' [John 1:14].

When we walk in grace and truth, we become sanctified, where the word *sanctify* in Greek means 'to make holy' [1 Peter 1:13-17+22-23; 1 Corinthians 3:17].

Jesus prayed to his Father and asked,

'*Sanctify them through thy truth: thy word is truth.*' [John 17:17]

We are justified when born-again, being cleansed from our former sins, and receive the Holy Spirit to help us on our journey of sanctification by living his word or his truth. Paul teaches that this process of sanctification comes through walking in the commandments given by Jesus,

'*Furthermore then we beseech you, brethren, and exhort you by the Lord Jesus, that as ye have received of us how ye ought to walk and to please God, so ye would abound more and more. For ye know what commandments we gave you by the Lord Jesus. For this is the will of God, even your sanctification, that ye should abstain from …*' [1 Thessalonians 4:1-9]

He then gives examples of things we should abstain from, such as fornication, lust, fraud, uncleanness, etc. and reminds us that we should '*love one another*' as Jesus taught. This is the process of sanctification, which we cannot do alone. We need the redemptive power of Jesus to help sanctify us through his blood, as it is written, '*Wherefore Jesus also, that he might sanctify the people with his own blood, suffered [outside] the gate [of Jerusalem].*' [Hebrews 13:12]

Interestingly, we are to help the process of sanctification by purging ourselves from unclean things, such as fleeing from youthful lusts and following righteousness, faith, charity, peace, etc. [2 Timothy 2:21-22].

Throughout the Old Testament, the Lord says, '*Sanctify yourselves*', which was first given in Leviticus,

'*Sanctify yourselves therefore, and be ye holy: for I am the Lord your God. And ye shall keep my statutes, and do them: I am the Lord which sanctify you.'* [Leviticus 20:7-8; 11:44]

So the process of sanctification is not a one-way street, as demonstrated by Jesus time and time again when he tells us to forgive others, or we will not be forgiven, or to clothe the naked, or feed the hungry, or visit those in prison [Matthew 25:35-40]. Jesus repeatedly taught what we must do to help sanctify ourselves but never said we are doing this alone. His grace strengthens us, as Paul taught,

'*I can do all things through Christ which strengtheneth me*' [Philippians 4:13].

We become sanctified by following the Holy Spirit [Galatians 5:22-23]. Indeed, the Holy Spirit plays a vital role in this process, empowering us to be obedient to the truth [1 Peter 1:2; 2 Thessalonians 2:13]. Eventually, Jesus will sanctify us once he sees that we are willing to suffer all tribulations and trials in his name [Galatians 5:24-25].

We are sanctified by grace when we learn to show grace to others. When we save others in the small sense of the word, through being a good Samaritan, we wash our robes in the blood of Christ [Revelation 7:14], enabling him to sanctify us in the large sense of the word, grace for grace. God will freely forgive our former sins and then help sanctify us, making us holy, when we show grace to others, but restore our former sins if we fail to follow his example of grace [Matthew 18:32-35; Ephesians 4:32].

Once we have been saved from our sins, we are commanded to walk in the light of his truth.

'Grace be with you, mercy, and peace, from God the Father, and from the Lord Jesus Christ, the Son of the Father, in truth and love. I rejoiced greatly that I found of thy children walking in truth, as we have received a commandment from the Father ... And this is love, that we walk after his commandments. This is the commandment, That, as ye have heard from the beginning, ye should walk in it.' [2 John 1:3-6].

Over time, people have changed God's comm<u>a</u>ndments to become his comm<u>e</u>ndments. They would commend anyone to walk after his truth but never say he commanded them to do so. This great lie only requires you to change one letter in the commandments, but Jesus warned against changing even the tiniest part,

'For verily I say unto you, Till heaven and earth pass, one jot or one tittle shall in no wise pass from the law, till all be fulfilled. Whosoever therefore shall break one of these least commandments, and shall teach men so, he shall be called the least in the kingdom of heaven: but whosoever shall do and teach them, the same shall be called great in the kingdom of heaven' [Matthew 5:18-19].

When we repent and accept Jesus as our Lord and Saviour, we know our former sins are washed away, which is *justification* through his grace. We are then commanded to walk after his commandments so that we might become holy, which is *sanctification* through grace and truth [1 John 3:3; 1 Peter 1:16+22].

Welcome to 'Grace for Grace'

PART I

Alpha: Harnessing Grace

To Eva
1815

Content

Prologue

The symbol of a fish was used by early Christians as a sign of their faith when persecution meant it was challenging to discuss openly the tenets of their belief. An old story tells of two men who met on a dusty road; one drew half an arc in the dirt while the other drew the opposite arc to complete the sign. I have met fellow Christians who would say that my faith in Christ was upside down. On one such occasion, as we spoke on our symbolic dirt road, we both drew our arcs and realised some enlightening truths about Christ. We each asked ourselves, have I really been born-again? No matter from which side up we look at the fish, whether from the side of grace or the side of discipleship, it is still the same fish.

The good news of the Gospel is that we will all be resurrected, whether good or evil. The additional good news is that all who have sinned and repented, calling upon the name of Jesus Christ, will be forgiven of their past sins (saved). The gospel also reminds us that we will stand at the judgment bar of Christ, and it will be done unto us according to the parable of the talents and the pounds (reward).

Before and during Jesus' life, the Law of Moses (the law of works) was the standard everyone should have kept but struggled to live. After Jesus' death, there was much confusion about whether they should continue to live the law of works that Moses taught. There were disputations about whether new Christians should be circumcised as stated in the law, which arguments centred around Jewish converts who wanted Gentiles to live the law of Moses.

While arguments about whether they should keep the works of Moses were settled in Acts chapter 15, the disputations rumbled on for years and are the subject of many of Paul's epistles. He argued strongly that the law of Moses does not save us, but salvation comes by faith in Jesus Christ and detailed how a person's life changes when they are living by faith, not by the works of the law. He said that if we think the law of Moses saves us, then Christ (the Messiah) died in vain [Galatians 2:21].

Nowadays, the definition of works has taken on an entirely different meaning because we are not surrounded by those who were raised as Jews and in a different historical setting. We have lost the context. Often, we mistake not being saved by works as meaning we don't need to follow any of Jesus' teachings anymore, but just say we believe he is the miracle cure. Even getting baptised is considered a pointless 'work' to some Christians.

We will address these issues by likening our discipleship to a person climbing a large rock wall, which metaphor will become an integral part of the book. Please imagine you are a new Christian feeling out of place and overwhelmed as you read the following parable.

Parable of the Clip

Towering above me at dawn stands the rock, tall and dominating. Behind me, two dusty red graves lay empty. I look up and see jagged extrusions, cracks and crevices: my path of painful progression. The journey had been easy until now, passing by smooth portions of the wall with no handgrips, where people were happy and socialising, but they hardly noticed me when I walked by. As the sun rises in the east, I see the start of the route that must be taken but cannot see where the sides of the wall end or how far up it goes. Beside me is a rope that descends from above, and inside my soul is a knowledge that I must climb. At chest height, hung on the wall, is my harness.

Others are on the bouldering wall behind me, climbing the short distance to the top. They do not need the harness as the promised landing mats at the bottom are there to break their fall. The schoolmaster in attendance tells them exactly where to place each hand as they climb, but some choose to walk from that place towards where I now stand. I turn to face the upward abyss once more.

Legend has it that a climber free-soloed the rock wall many years ago and placed the cyan rope at the top to help those who followed him. Some say he created the wall. No one has ever reached the top without his rope. The word is, he came down to tell climbers how to use the rope and instruct them to put on the harnesses but then returned and lives in a city so high up it must surely touch the heavens. I long to go there.

Many of us stand at the rocky wall with stories and advice for each other. '*Ignore the rope,*' some say, '*we all have our own path to follow*', but I know that only one climber has made it. To the left and right are other ropes, colourful and bright, but they don't go all the way up. I reach out and take the red harness, trying to work out which foot goes in where, but still put it on back to front. It felt wrong, so I turned it around. '*What are you wearing that for?*' came a mocking question from a passing climber. '*You don't need to wear the harness; it will restrict your movements.*' He shook his head and moved to a large group in the distance. Another climber gives me a comforting smile. We both knew we needed the harness and shared how grateful we were for the master climber who had shown us the way.

Opening the magenta carabineer on the harness, I clipped it to the rope. My new friend looks across, puzzled. '*Why have you done that?*' she asks. Surprised, I explained that because the master climber had placed a rope for us to use, I needed to be attached to it. Her countenance falls as she puts forward that the rope was just there to show us the way symbolically. She encourages me to have faith in his graceful harness alone. '*All you have to do is wear the harness,*' she said. '*The master climber will know you are there*'. I pause momentarily and question myself but feel peace when I see my clip attached to the rope.

Cautiously, I start to climb; it is awkward. The harness is comforting, yet my coordination is clumsy. The rope does not pull me up, so I have to climb. I am reassured that should I fall, I am safe in his harness and will not fall far.

As I continue upward, I see a large group of people at the base wearing harnesses and singing praise to the Free Soloist. A fellow climber tells me they do not need to climb the rock because the master has done it for them, and when the night comes, they believe he will collect them. They speak of the harness with great joy. In the gathering, I see a friend who looks up at me. Having learned a few things as I climb, I call down with advice for him.

'*Take the climbing shoes; they will help you grip. Take the helmet, too; it will protect you from falling rocks. Put on the chalk bag, and bring some chocolate!*'

Joyfully, I see him clip to the rope.

As the top approaches, dusk draws in, and I feel the need to hasten my climb. Remaining clipped on can be frustrating as I have to hold onto the rock with one hand and pull through the rope with the other. It is tempting to disconnect and clip back on later up the wall. I resist the urge. There is peace in knowing I am securely attached. Soon, it will be dark when no progress will be made. I am thankful for the Free Soloist and the rope he provided to show us the way. I am grateful for the harness and the clip. Pressing onwards and upwards, I try to use every last drop of the sun's light before it sets over the ridge. [John 9:4; Ephesians 4:7-15; Psalm 62]

Chapter One

The Free Soloist

Someone who climbs with no rope or safety equipment to catch them if they fall.

'... how grateful we were for the master climber who had shown us the way.'

As a child, I attended church and often saw a stained-glass version of Jesus depicted on windows or paintings. The image that endured for me was of a sad-looking figure hanging on a cross with a halo above his head. I had a knowledge of Christ but had yet to get to know him. My experience of church was repetitive and dull except for an excellent Sunday School teacher called Joan, who made the scriptures a little more straightforward and more relevant to me. When I turned eleven, I stopped attending.

My understanding was enlightened at age sixteen when my sister taught me who Jesus Christ was and shattered the stained-glass image I grew up with. She introduced me to the story of a young man who got into debt but for whom the due date was so far off that he did not give much heed to the burden he carried. After some small instalments and much time wasted, the due date fell, and the man did not make the payment. The young debtor pleaded for mercy and an extension of the loan's terms, but the creditor, to whom the money was owed, demanded that justice be done and payment made in full. Debtors' prison loomed on the horizon, and repossession of property was at the door. One man demanded justice while the other asked for mercy, and neither could be reconciled.

At this point, a friend of the debtor entered who knew of the young man's flawed nature and desperate situation. He turned to the creditor and said that he would meet the demands of justice by paying the debt in full on the young man's behalf. The friend then turned to the debtor and asked if he would agree to have him as his new creditor. In tears, the young man accepted. All three left with the demands of justice and mercy fully satisfied. [summation of B. K. Packer]

This story opened my eyes, and the morning star began to dawn in my soul. Justice was an eternal principle that could not be ignored, not even by God himself. We needed a merciful friend who could pay the price for our sins. We are all flawed with imperfections, no matter how hard we try. I understood that I was a debtor, and the Redeemer was my friend who had been keeping watch over my foolish nature throughout my life. There is a debt to be paid for our sins that our own efforts cannot meet. The laws of eternity require us to be thrown into a debtors' prison, where the price for our sins would be extracted, leaving us desolate [Matthew 18:29–35; 23:38]. How these laws are enacted and enforced is outside of our current understanding, but as children trust their parents when born into this world, we trust our Father in Heaven and his plan to satisfy the demands of justice when we leave.

Imagine if you had committed a crime and your own Father were the chief justice in the land. He would still have to uphold justice, or he would cease to be a judge. However, in his compassion and mercy, he would do all he could to mitigate the punishment. In the case of humanity's weaknesses, our loving Father and chief judge has provided a way for our sins to be taken upon the shoulders of his Son, our Saviour. If God brushed aside justice, he would cease to be a 'just' God, so the punishments must remain, but he can allow another to volunteer to pay the price [1 Peter 3:18].

Our Saviour has been known by many names in history, of which the following are just a few: Christ (English), Messiah (Hebrew), Christos (Greek), Son of David, Son of Man, Son of God, Redeemer of Israel, Emmanuel, Holy One of Israel, Mighty One of Jacob, Prince of Peace and Jesus. Each name carries a meaning to help us understand who he is. The most significant title he holds (for me) is 'The Lamb of God'. He volunteered to come to the Earth as a sacrificial lamb, to take the demands of justice upon himself.

As a Christian, it is essential to know his nature to understand our relationship with him and his role in our lives.

Before His Birth

We know our Father and his Son lived in heaven before the world was created. In the book of Genesis, we read, '*And God said, Let us make man in our image, after our likeness*' [Genesis 1:26]. John reminds us, '*In the beginning was the Word, and the Word was with God, and the Word was God. The same was in the beginning with God*' [John 1:1–2]. Just before Jesus suffered for our sins in the Garden of Gethsemane, he expressed his desire to return to live with the Father, residing in the same glory they had shared before creating the Earth. '*And now, O Father, glorify thou me with thine own self with the glory which I had with thee before the world was.*' [John 17:5] Jesus played a pivotal role in the creation of the world on which we now stand [Hebrews 1:1–2]; he created our physical bodies [Genesis 1:26] and volunteered to come to the Earth to pay the debt for our sins because of his love.

His Birth

Jesus was born, famously, to Mary, while Joseph the Carpenter became his earthly stepfather. Sometimes, when I consider the parentage of Jesus, I hear the introduction to 'You're Welcome' from Moana going around my head, with Maui, the demi-god, singing about the creation. It's a fun song, so please forgive my levity. More real than Percy Jackson and purer than Orion, Jesus lived upon the Earth as the only true demi-God (meaning a heavenly Father and a mortal mother), the Son of the Highest [Luke 1:32] and a God in his own right [Hebrews 1:8-10].

At the time of Jesus' birth, we know from the Gospel of Luke [chapter 2] that shepherds visited him. A new star appeared, which the Gospel of Matthew tells us led wise men to seek him out, although, contrary to the school nativities we watch, they did not arrive until Jesus was older, perhaps up to two years old. Matthew 2:7–11 tells us he was a young child rather than a baby when the wise men arrived and that he was living in a house by then. Matthew only talks about the wise men who visited the young boy, whereas Luke mentions the shepherds who visited the baby. The Gospels of Mark and John do not address the Nativity at all. Often, we learn that popular narratives are not always correct.

After the wise men left, Jesus' family went to Egypt to be safe from the wicked King Herod, just as the infant Moses had been saved in Egypt by the daughter of Pharaoh. This is only one of the many parallels between the lives of Moses and Jesus [Deuteronomy 18:15; Acts 3:22]. After his family returned from Egypt upon the death of Herod, they settled in Nazareth.

It is stated that Jesus was a son of David:

'*The book of the generation of Jesus Christ, the son of David, the son of Abraham.*' [Matthew 1:1]

So, Jesus was a descendant of the king of Israel.

If Israel had not slipped into rebellion and ceased to function as a viable kingdom when Jerusalem was captured in 587 BC then we may have seen Jesus sitting on the throne of King David. It has been suggested that

Mary and Joseph had royal blood, with Mary possibly being a first cousin to Joseph or a first cousin once removed (see works by Lord A. Hervey and Steven Donald Norris, respectively). If so, the promise to David came to pass, not only through Jesus' adoption by his stepfather but also through the earthly bloodline of his mother.

'*Therefore being a prophet, and knowing that God had sworn with an oath to [David], that of the fruit of his loins, according to the flesh, he would raise up Christ to sit on his throne.*' [Acts 2:30; Revelation 22:16]

His Rejection

When Jesus rode into Jerusalem on a donkey to symbolise he was the prince of peace, the people shouted '*Hosanna*', which means '*Save now*'. They knew Jesus was fulfilling the prophecy in Zachariah,

'*Behold, thy King cometh unto thee: he is just, and having salvation; lowly, and riding upon an ass, and upon a colt the foal of an ass.*' [Zechariah 9:9]

The people, therefore, hailed him as their king with the expectation that he would subdue the Romans and take back their city. They grew disillusioned when it became apparent he would not provide a military solution to the vassalage of Rome. Soon, instead of hailing him, Jesus was condemned by the very people he had come to free from sin.

The sign written above the cross was correct on both a physical and spiritual level: 'JESUS OF NAZARETH THE KING OF THE JEWS.' (INRI) [John 19:19–22] If Jesus just wanted followers, he could have raised up people from the stones to follow him [Matthew 3:9], but, in modern terms, he is not seeking 'likes' or 'hearts' on social media. Jesus wants us to be his disciples by taking up our crosses and following his teachings. We should not fall into the trap of the people in his time and expect salvation by simply crying '*Hosanna!*' [John 12:13]

His Suffering and Death

After baptism, Jesus went into the wilderness to fast for forty days and nights. Along with his bodily suffering, he experienced temptations designed to make him question his divine role as our Saviour and unsettle him from his mission. He overcame these initial trials and went on to experience even greater tests at the end of his mortal ministry. When Jesus suffered for our sins in the 'olive press' known as the Garden of Gethsemane, he would have experienced every pain we have endured and felt every mental and physical sickness [Isaiah 53:3-5]. Even though he was prepared to experience this suffering, it is written that he was '*sore amazed*' at what he had to endure as his sweat, like blood, fell in large drops from his body [Luke 22:44]. That night, in agony, the Son of God met the demands of justice head-on.

Jesus was betrayed by Judas and taken away by the guards. He was scourged with Roman lashes, almost to the point of death, then led to his crucifixion. Darkness came at the sixth hour, and then, about the ninth (3 pm), he cried out loudly, feeling forsaken by God. After being offered vinegar to drink and crying out one more time, he finished his suffering and allowed himself to die [Matthew 27:46–50]. There is no pain, sorrow or feeling of abandonment we can pass through which he has not first suffered himself. Because of his suffering, we can trust his judgments and turn to him for rest and comfort in our own afflictions. [Hebrews 2:18; Malachi 4:2]

His Resurrection and Physical Form

When Jesus was resurrected, he appeared in the same form—that of a man—as he had done during his mortal life. He ate fish and honey, looked like a man and could touch things. In the Gospel of Luke, he told his disciples to,

'*[touch] me, and see; for a spirit hath not flesh and bones, as you see me have*' [Luke 24:39].

The physical nature of Jesus was not taught to me as a child. Many suggested God was a powerful cloud, and it would be wrong for us to confine him to a body of flesh and bone. A closer reading of this scripture, however, teaches that although the room was shut, his physical body was not restricted from passing through the closed doors into their midst [John 20:26; Luke 24:36-37]. Jesus was keen to demonstrate he was not just a spirit, but his spirit had now united with an immortal physical body. We will also receive a physical body like Jesus, as all people will be resurrected [Philippians 3:20-21; 1 Corinthians 15:20-22].

Paul suggests that God and Jesus look similar:

'*In whom we have redemption through his blood, even the forgiveness of sins: Who is the image of the invisible God, the firstborn of every creature.*' [Colossians 1:14–16]

Note: The Greek word used for *image* (1504) means '*bust*', or '*likeness*', such as you see in a museum.

Hebrews is a little more specific regarding these similarities,

'*Who being the brightness of his glory, and the express image of his person.*' [Hebrews 1:3]

When we realise that we look like Jesus, who looks like his Father, we can see more clearly the divine potential within each of us to become more like them [Matthew 5:48].

Prophets have communicated with the Lord face-to-face throughout history.

'*And the Lord spake unto Moses face to face, as a man speaketh unto his friend.*' [Exodus 24:9–12; 33:11; Job 42:5–6; Genesis 32:30]

Growing up, I had a mental image of a cosmic intelligence, a sort of cloud-like God who created everything. Knowing that God the Father and his Son are in the express image of each other and that we, too, are created in their image made it easier for me to know why they love us so much. My children, created in my image (*likeness*), are of untold and unspeakable value to me. If I can love my children as much as I do, then my Heavenly Father can love me, not just as a pot of clay that he fashioned, but with a genuine paternal and eternal love that surpasses my understanding. His love is unconditional and, therefore, not dependent upon us believing in him.

At his ascension into heaven from the Mount of Olives, those who witnessed it were instructed by two angels that Jesus shall appear in the same way at his second coming.

'*Ye men of Galilee, why stand ye gazing up into heaven? this same Jesus, which is taken up from you into heaven, shall so come in like manner as ye have seen him go into heaven*' [Acts 1:10–11 (up); Zechariah 14:4 (down)].

It is essential to know who we worship. From the accounts of those who beheld the Lord face to face and from his appearance to over 500 disciples at once [1 Corinthians 15:6], we know that we can have faith in the resurrected Lord and love him with all our hearts. While he certainly has a spirit, and we must worship him in spirit and truth, he has demonstrated through an empty tomb that his physical, resurrected body (which houses his spirit) is as real as you or I. Countless wolves in untold flocks have gradually chipped away at the image of God to form their own graven image. Still, the picture that the Free Soloist painted for us remains visible today for all who have eyes to see and ears to hear [see Romans 11:8].

- ✓ We are created in his image
- ✓ He is in the image of God
- ✓ We can speak to him as we do with a friend
- ✓ He is now a resurrected being with flesh and bone
- ✓ He is the king of Israel who will come again
- ✓ He loves us

Chapter Two

His Perfect Ascent

'Legend has it that a free climber soloed the wall many years ago ... No other has ever reached the top on their own.'

When at school, I thought it strange that if you took any number and multiplied it by zero, the answer was always zero. I figured that if I had twenty to begin with and then multiplied it by zero, I would still have twenty, but this proved false. Only if I multiplied twenty by one would I end up with my original twenty. The same principle applies to the sins of mankind. No matter how sincere and full of love a man may be, even if he had only one sin and tried to take upon himself the sins of the world, the whole world's sins multiplied by his single sin would still leave the same number. The only way to delete sin and forgive a person is to multiply their sins by zero, which is why Jesus needed to be a man free from transgression. He had to be the lamb without blemish as he was the great and last sacrifice.

The Old Testament is full of sacrifices. The first animal sacrifice recorded is in Genesis when Abel (son of Adam) offered the firstling of his flock [Genesis 4:4]. This practice continued with God's people from Adam to the time of Christ. Moses instituted a law that required a detailed list of sacrifices, such as those at the feast of

Passover, which had seen thousands upon thousands of lambs offered by the priests on behalf of the people's sins. As mentioned earlier, we often hear Jesus Christ referred to as 'The Lamb of God', as this title is perhaps the best explanation of his role as our Saviour and Redeemer. The law of Moses was set up as a schoolmaster [Galatians 3:24–25] to bring people to understand the need for a Saviour who could and would redeem them from their sins. When the people of God sacrificed a lamb, they should have had in mind the reason for the symbol, which was that—in their future—there would be a final sacrifice, even the Messiah Jesus Christ.

John the Baptist referenced the sin offerings made at the feast of Passover when he declared, '*Behold the lamb of God which taketh away the sins of the world*'. Paul mentioned this role, saying, '*For even Christ, our Passover is sacrificed for us*', and Peter, to whom the keys of the Kingdom were given, declared, '... *But with the precious blood of Christ, as of a lamb without blemish and without spot*'. Each lamb sacrificed was to be as perfect as possible, without defects or marks and had to be the firstborn. Jesus Christ had zero sins and was the firstborn of Mary; therefore, he was able to offer himself on our behalf.

Quick aside: *One job of the shepherds keeping watch over their flocks was to witness which lambs were the 'firstborn' to their mothers. This was done so that the law could be fulfilled, requiring only the firstborn to be offered as a sacrifice upon the altar. Knowing this, we can understand why the shepherds were selected to be the first visitors of the newborn baby. Not only* *was Jesus to be a shepherd to us all, but he was witnessed as the 'firstborn' by those appointed to this responsibility in ancient times. The shepherds in Bethlehem were historically those who looked after the Temple flock and would have witnessed the birth of lambs offered on behalf of the people in the Temple. These shepherds would wrap the new male lambs in swaddling bands to protect them from blemishes or breaking any bones in their early days. The following year, they would be offered at the Temple.*

To help us understand that offering His Son for our sins was not a simple 'tick in the box' exercise for the Father, we were given the earthly example of Abraham and Isaac to demonstrate the gravity of the sacrifice. When Abraham finally had his firstborn child with Sarah, he was amazed and overjoyed. Isaac was a blessing for which they had indeed given up hope and came to Abraham and Sarah in the twilight of their years. One day—when Isaac was old enough to assist his father in the daily chores and understand the law—Abraham received a commandment that tested his faith to the core. He was to go up a mountain in the land of Moriah [Genesis 22:2] and offer his beloved son as a sacrifice. Can you imagine the feeling in Abraham's heart when he heard this command? How heavy would he have been during the three-day journey towards the mount? This terrible test of faith ended when Abraham was about to lift up the knife and offer his son.

'And Abraham stretched forth his hand, and took the knife to slay his son. And the angel of the Lord called unto him out of heaven, and said, Abraham, Abraham: and he said, Here am I. And he said, Lay not thine hand upon the lad, neither do thou any thing unto him: for now I know that

thou fearest God, seeing thou hast not withheld thy son, thine only son from me. And Abraham lifted up his eyes, and looked, and behold behind him a ram caught in a thicket by his horns: and Abraham went and took the ram, and offered him up for a burnt offering in the stead of his son.' [Genesis 22:10–13]

The relief of Abraham (and, indeed, Isaac) at this time must have been immense, but the whole experience taught a profound lesson. Not only did God reveal the strength of Abraham's faithfulness, but Abraham, the father of many nations, had experienced to some degree the heartache that our Father in heaven would feel when he was to offer for a sacrifice his unique birthright Son. Abraham's test impresses upon each of us the suffering our Father in heaven (our chief judge) endured when he offered his Son upon the altar.

The offering of lambs and rams is symbolic, but God wanted to give us the proper and painful reason for the symbol.

'*For God so loved the world, that he gave his only begotten Son, that whosoever believeth in him should not perish, but have everlasting life.*' [John 3:16]

Billy Graham declared that this verse represents 'The Greatest Love Story Ever Told'. It surely does.

Jesus spoke about the pain and suffering he was to endure for our sins.

'*And they came to a place which was named Gethsemane: and he saith to his disciples, Sit ye here, while I shall pray. And he taketh with him Peter and James and John, and began to be sore amazed, and to be very heavy; And saith unto them, My soul is exceeding sorrowful unto death: tarry ye here, and watch. And he went forward a little, and fell on the ground, and prayed that, if it were possible, the hour might pass from him. And he said, Abba, Father, all things are possible unto thee; take away this cup from me: nevertheless not what I will, but what thou wilt.*' [Mark 14:32–36]

From his expression, we see the emotion and humanity of this pivotal moment in the history of humankind. Jesus didn't need forgiveness. The reason for his suffering was to fulfil the mission given to him by the Father because of the love he had for God and his love for each of us. It was the turning point of Earth's existence from being a fallen sphere with lost and fallen people to a hopeful place of faith and a bright future. Humanity was hanging in the balance, not by the calculations of a robot, but by the painful, gritty determination of a divine man who came from God to suffer on our behalf and deliver us from eternal darkness. The suffering of the Messiah is set forth here, but Abraham embodied the anguish of his Father nearly 2,000 years earlier.

Jesus did not have to bear the weight of our sins in Gethsemane. He had the power to summon more than twelve legions of angels (over 72,000) to rescue him from the cross, yet he chose not to. Instead, he drank the bitter cup his Father had prepared for him out of love for each of us. No words in any human language can fully capture the depth of suffering he willingly endured, a sacrifice that should fill us with a profound sense of gratitude.

There is an eternal law by which we are admitted into God's presence. Justice must be fulfilled, but it can only be satisfied by the merits and mercy of Jesus. He is our advocate with the Father, who pleads our case, almost like a lawyer acting on our behalf.

'*...if any man sin, we have an advocate with the Father, Jesus Christ the righteous: And he is the propitiation for our sins: and not for ours only, but also for the sins of the whole world. And hereby we do know that we know him, if we keep his commandments.*' [1 John 2:1–6]

Why did Christ have to die for us? To satisfy the law of justice that governs the heavens. A lamb without blemish needed to suffer through the pains and agonies caused by the sins of all mankind to the point that the scales of heavenly justice could be overpowered through the weight of his mercy. Thus, he can stand before the eternal judge and grant mercy to those who have chosen him as their advocate. No other person has so perfectly free soloed the ascent of life. We all depended on the master climber to throw us the rope, and he delivered!

Chapter Three

The Fall

'Two dusty red graves lay empty'

– A reference to Adam and Eve

Most people are gifted with a simple skill of discernment: We can tell the difference between a child who looks us in the eye, shouts 'SORRY!' then slams the bedroom door, and the one who looks at their feet and softly speaks the same word.

The Saviour is not a doormat upon whom we wipe our feet after playing in the world of sin. The atonement of Jesus Christ—which describes his suffering, death, and resurrection—liberates us from the original transgression. It is through the atonement that we are freed from Adam's fall and the curse of permanent physical death. Even the most hardened of sinners will be resurrected. Paul taught,

'*As in Adam all die, even so in Christ, shall all be made alive.*' [1 Cor. 15:22]

By God's grace, every person, regardless of their worthiness, will be given the gift of resurrection. Adam's fall was not our fault, and God, in his justice, does not hold us accountable for it. The crucial point is that Jesus' atonement also covers individual sins, for which we can only blame ourselves, through the process known as 'repentance'.

Forgiveness is required to redeem us from our falls, but it is not an automatic gift like the resurrection. In times past, people have said that all you need to do to be forgiven is say you believe in Jesus. However, our Lord said twice in short succession,

'*I tell you, Nay: but, except ye repent, ye shall all likewise perish… I tell you, Nay: but, except ye repent, ye shall all likewise perish.*' [Luke 13:3–5]

Damnation

When the scriptures speak of '*perishing*', as in the example above, it has reference to a spiritual death, which is the separation of our spirits from God. An excellent way to imagine spiritual death is like a dam built across a river, which stops the water from progressing. The water is dammed! When we speak of damnation, we refer to the separation of man from God spiritually insomuch that their progression back to him is blocked. Judgment Day is when we meet the dam, and none of us on earth can make it past without sincere repentance and the grace of God, which grants us permission to go through the sluice gates and enjoy the open water of God's heavenly city. It is interesting to me that, because of Adam, 'a-dam' was placed between humanity and God. The Lord has removed the physical blockage put there by our first parents, but we each continue to block our own progression by the sins of our own volition. Freedom from sin through repentance allows us to flow freely back to God, who gave us life.

Some may worry that keeping the commandments is restrictive and hinders us from living life to the fullest. However, they can be assured that God's people will be the freest of all the children of men! Just like the child who flies a kite, we may want to let go of the string, thinking it holds the kite back from going higher, not realizing that the very string which holds it down, keeps it aloft. We can choose our sins, but we cannot choose their eternal consequences.

Quick aside: *The word 'atonement' in English means 'At-one-ment', where two things that were separated are brought back together, such as our spirits and bodies being reunited, as well as being reunited with our God when we are brought back into his presence. When we have sinned, we ask for the grace of Jesus Christ to cover our sin. In Hebrew, the word for atonement is 'Kaphar', which means to 'cover'. In this regard, think of Jesus covering our sins by burying them in the tomb with him or in the waters of baptism, wherein we are covered by water and washed. It is also appropriate to remember that the LORD God made coats of skin to 'cover' Adam and Eve after their transgression in the Garden of Eden [Genesis 3:21]. We are not told how these skins were obtained, but if it were by sacrificing an animal, it would be the first time a sacrifice was made to cover, or atone, for mankind symbolically.*

Remember that the Old Testament law required a lamb to be offered on a regular basis. Now that the Lord Jesus has offered himself as a great and last sacrifice for sin, what must we do to be partakers of his heavenly gift of forgiveness? What is the offering we should now make to the Lord?

Repentance

In Greek, the word for repentance is *metanoia* (3341), which means 'a change of mind' or 'a change of your inner person'. Psalms is a great place to learn about this change-offering we make to the Lord. Jesus often quoted the Psalms, so we know he held them in high regard. The Old Testament is the Old Covenant, but by no means should this wonderful book be overlooked [Matthew 13:52]. It was the bedrock of Jesus' teaching and pointed to him in every way. The book of Psalms tells us:

'*The Lord is nigh unto them that are of a broken heart; and saveth such as be of a contrite spirit*' [Psalm 34:18].

A '*broken heart*' speaks of the godly sorrow we feel for sins committed in our lives and the regrets we have accumulated. Before a farmer can plant a seed, he must *break* the soil, usually done with a plough that cuts deep into the ground, preparing a place for the seed and helping irrigation. Once the seed is planted, the ground is harrowed up, which grinds lumps of soil into a powder-like texture, helping to remove weeds and cover the seeds. Similar to harrowing, the Hebrew word for '*contrite*' means '*ground to dust*'.

In the parables, we learn that the sower is Jesus, the seed is the gospel, and our hearts are the soil [Matthew 13:3-9]. Hence, we must have the soil of our hearts broken in humility, enabling the gospel to grow inside us and our minds harrowed up to help remove lumps of soil and weeds. We can then bring forth fruit appropriate for repentance [Matthew 3:8]. The harrowing begins once the seed is planted, but Jesus can remove the pain if we call out to him. He helps us through the growth process, strengthening us with his enabling grace.

Repentance is not a free credit card from God to pay off old sins and purchase new ones at will. Even when we have been born-again, we still make mistakes, but those transgressions should not be met with thoughts of 'Oh well, I will be forgiven', but rather, 'I feel bad for making a mistake'. The feeling of a '*broken heart*' and '*contrite spirit*' should lead to a phoenix mentality where one is born-again from the ashes. This makes the phrase '*sackcloth and ashes*' more understandable when used in the symbolic context of repentance [Daniel 9:3–5]. 'Godly sorrow' is regret for the sin committed, whereas 'Manly sorrow' is regret you got caught.

This principle of repentance is expressed by David when he had sinned a grievous sin and was wrestling with God in mighty prayer for forgiveness,

'*Hide thy face from my sins, and blot out all mine iniquities. Create in me a clean heart, O God; and renew a right spirit within me. Cast me not away from thy presence, and take not thy holy spirit from me. For thou desirest not sacrifice; else would I give it: thou delightest not in burnt offering. The sacrifices of God are a broken spirit: a broken and a contrite heart.*' [Psalm 51:9–19 shortened]

Through the expression of a '*broken and a contrite heart*', he shows that Old Testament prophets were well aware their sacrificing of animals would be to no avail if their hearts were not right before God. Animal sacrifices were designed to remind them of the Messiah, who would come to take away their sins, but what God wanted in return was a change in people's hearts, to move them away from sin entirely. Confessing with our mouths that we believe in Jesus is not the last tick in the box on our journey back to heaven, but only the first. Next is to have our very hearts changed and our spirits brought in line with the Lord. He has described the type of people who will dwell in the glory of heaven with him by saying,

'*For thus saith the high and lofty One that inhabiteth eternity, whose name is Holy; I dwell in the high and holy place, with him also that is of a contrite and humble spirit, to revive the spirit of the humble, and to revive the heart of the contrite ones*' [Isaiah 57:15].

While the Old Testament describes how we should feel about repentance, the New Testament describes the practicalities of what we should do today. The Elders and Chief Priests in the New Testament asked many questions designed to entrap Jesus, so he used parables to teach the principles of righteousness in a manner that cannot be denied by a reasonable person, no matter what their faith may be. On one occasion, he taught the following:

'*But what think ye? A certain man had two sons; and he came to the first, and said, Son, go work today in my vineyard. He answered and said, I will not: but afterward he repented, and went. And he came to the second, and said likewise. And he answered and said, I go, sir: and went not. [Which] of them ... did the will of his Father? They say unto him, The first. Jesus saith unto them, Verily I say unto you, That the publicans and the harlots go into the kingdom of God before you.*' [Matthew 21:28–31]

When a person genuinely accepts Jesus as their Lord and Saviour through repentance, they then 'go' and practice doing the will of the Father. A person who is not genuine will say that they will do the work, but will not do it, and become a Sunday morning Christian. What did Jesus say was the consequence of paying lip service to him at the end of that last parable?

Regardless of our previous decisions, the life-changing process of repentance can mean our final destination is determined by our choices of today and not by those of the past. A child learning to ride a bike may fall off multiple times, but each attempt is one step closer to their goal of confidently riding the bike alone. So it is with our journey to becoming like the Lord. We may often fail to live up to his standard, but if we repent and get back up when we fall, our sins will not be abject failures but stepping stones along the path to perfection. Our time on earth is the time to repent and grow, as there are no stabilisers on bikes in the kingdom of heaven. For someone who honestly repents, Judgment Day is not about asking how many times they fell off, but rather, have they learned to ride the bike!

C. S. Lewis was the most significant Christian apologist of the 20th century, writing many books that people still love today. In his work 'The Screwtape Letters', the main protagonist explained to his nephew, Wormwood, how God feels about our failings,

'*He wants them to learn to walk and must therefore take away His hand; and if only the will to walk is really there he is pleased even with their stumbles.*'

Our Father in Heaven loves to help us learn to walk. He reaches down and picks us up when we cry to him. It is a sure tactic of the adversary to make us feel that our mistakes are final versions of ourselves; however, we would do well to retort back with the old saying: 'Judge me not, for I am not yet a finished product.'

I like the thought that the Hebrew word for 'sin' (*chata* 2398) and the corresponding Greek word (*hamartia* 266) indicate an arrow falling short of the centre of the target or missing the mark. We could use this analogy for golf, darts, football, or other goal-centred activities. While we all fall short of perfection, there is a difference between someone who aims and misses and someone who does not aim at all. Only one person in history has hit all their spiritual targets first time. In golfing terms, we could say that Jesus would always get a 'hole-in-one'. While we may not be on par with the Holy One, we can improve our game by being on his team and following his counsel.

The words of the master to Peter bring comfort when we fall short and sin again, '*Then came Peter to him, and said,*

Lord, how oft shall my brother sin against me, and I forgive him? till seven times? Jesus saith unto him, I say not unto thee, Until seven times: but, Until seventy times seven' [Matthew 18:21–22].

A repentant person would never calculate to sin 490 times, or they would not have been repentant in the first place. The lesson teaches us the principle of forgiveness, not just to others, but that we must be able to forgive ourselves.

A repentant person:

- Intends to follow the example of Christ
- Has Godly sorrow when they fall short
- Calls upon the Lord sincerely for forgiveness
- Demonstrates a change of heart.

The old dusty graves of Adam and Eve lay empty now. They have been resurrected and redeemed through the atonement of Jesus Christ. As we embark upon our own journey, it is comforting to know we are harnessed by the love of Jesus, who can forgive our sins when we fall short. Sin used to bring death and permanent separation from God, but now we have the hope of redemption in Christ, no matter how far we have fallen. Hope is the anchor to which the rope of Christ is attached [Hebrews 6:19].

Chapter Four

Dawn

'Towering above me at dawn stands the wall, tall and dominating ... inside my soul is a knowledge that I must climb'

A pure-blood friend and I had one of our conversations about Jesus, where we both drew our arcs in the dirt road. I felt I must believe in Jesus Christ to be saved from my sins and then strive to follow his teachings to become more like him. However, my friend suggested I only need to be saved once, and then I would be taken to heaven without the need to keep any commandments. He suggested that good people who have never been taught about Jesus would go to hell, and wicked people who have accepted Jesus but kept on sinning would go to heaven. This type of conversation was commonplace.

The famous 'born-again' phrase is a result of Jesus' encounter with Nicodemus the Pharisee in John chapter three. A Pharisee was a member of a particularly outwardly obedient group within the Jewish community. They gave strict heed to the 613 rules in the law of Moses and the oral law that grew up around it. They were happy to be seen speaking the word, while their hearts were often far from it. We are early into the story of Jesus, so the hostility that existed later among the Pharisees' is not present as Nicodemus openly confessed they knew God was with him. We don't know if Nicodemus had a specific question, but we do know Jesus taught him as follows:

'*Verily, verily, I say unto thee, Except a man be born again, he cannot* ***see*** *the kingdom of God. Nicodemus saith unto him, How can a man be born when he is old? Can he enter the second time into his mother's womb, and be born? Jesus answered, Verily, verily, I say unto thee, Except a man be born of water and of the Spirit, he cannot* ***enter*** *into the kingdom of God.*' [John 3:3–5]

Many people catch a glimpse of heaven and '*see*' (v.3) the kingdom during their first stage of being born-again when the light of Christ dawns upon them. You could say that this is the point at which they first 'see the light'. They must then make their journey towards that light. For some, just *see*ing the kingdom from afar is enough, and they choose to walk down other paths, feeling they have done all they need to be saved. However, Jesus then teaches that to '*enter*' (v.5) the kingdom of God a person must be '*born of water* <u>*and*</u> *of the spirit*' which requires us to do something more.

In Matthew, Jesus teaches that we '*enter*' the kingdom through a '*strait gate*', and not everyone who calls upon the Lord will enter through the gate, just like those who *see* the kingdom from afar but decide not to *enter*. The way we *enter* the kingdom is by doing the will of the Father.

'*Not every one that saith unto me, Lord, Lord, shall* <u>*enter*</u> *into the kingdom of heaven; but he that doeth the will of my Father which is in heaven.*' [Matthew 7:12-21]

Several steps enable us to experience this born-again process in our lives:

Step one: A person must have their hearts '*pricked*' by the Holy Spirit, where they catch a glimpse of heaven in their hearts and desire to go there. This is the first moment of the born-again process, a 'dawn' for the soul. [Acts 2:37-38]

Step two: A person then walks towards the kingdom by following the steps of the Saviour, who was baptised to show us the way [Acts 8:36-39]. This baptismal step includes repenting of old sins [Matthew 3:8].

Step three: They then receive the gift of the Holy Spirit, which—like a fire—helps to sanctify them spiritually. Both water and fire are spiritually significant in the cleansing process that not only washes our sins away but also purifies us to help remove the dross [Acts 19:6; Matthew 3:11–12; Proverbs 25:4]. This lifelong process of sanctification through following the fruits of the Holy Spirit is what is meant by '*doing the will of [the] Father which is in heaven*' and walking in his way of truth [Matthew 7:21; Galatians 5:18-25].

Quick aside: *When Adam was made flesh, the Lord breathed into him the breath of life [Genesis 2:7]. The act of breathing is called respiration, the first part being inspiration and the* *second, expiration. When we are born-again, we are inspired by the Holy Spirit [John 20:22].*

As we explore the scriptures associated with these three steps (a fourth is mentioned later), keeping some vital symbology in mind will be helpful. In the Old Testament, water reflected the need to be cleansed, so the law of Moses required frequent washing. When John was baptising in the River Jordan, the people flocked to him, which indicates the Jews at the time knew about the need for this type of cleansing. The religious fever surrounding John could be seen as the genuine First Great Awakening and troubled the Pharisees. Nobody questioned why water baptism was necessary as they washed symbolically, not just once in a lifetime, but whenever the need for cleansing arose. This ritual cleansing was known as 'Tevilah' in Judaism. It was usually performed in a 'Mikveh' (large bath) with fresh running water. We are born of water from the womb; the world was filled with water at the beginning of creation, and Noah and his family were all borne of water to start the human family again [1 Peter 3:20–21]. Our second birth follows the Saviour's example of being baptised in a place with much water [John 3:23].

Quick aside: *The person who took over from Moses to lead the children of Israel into the promised land after forty years in the wilderness was called 'Joshua'. The Hebrew name Joshua (Yehoshua or Yeshua) means 'Jehovah Saves'. The Greek form of Joshua is 'Iesous', which became 'Iesus' in Latin and then 'Jesus' in English. Joshua symbolically baptised the children of Israel as he led them through the River Jordan. Jesus led the way for us when he was baptised in the same river, most likely* *at the same crossing point Joshua used (Bethabara) to enter the promised land. Just as Joshua took over from Moses, so Jesus' law of faith took over from the law of Moses.*

***Note**: Some Christians believe water baptism is an optional part of the salvation process, which is addressed in the next book 'Distant Venom'.*

When Jesus asked Simon Peter who he believed he was, Peter replied, '*Thou art the Christ, the son of the living God*' [Matthew 16:16]. Jesus said he knew this because God revealed it to him [v. 17]. When this happens to us, the power of the Spirit reveals Jesus Christ is the Son of God [John 15:26]. The gift of the Holy Spirit had not descended upon the people while Jesus was ministering on earth [John 7:39] but was given by the apostles to the believers in Acts chapter two on the day of Pentecost [Acts 1:5; 2:1–4]. After this experience, people who were brought to a knowledge of the divinity of Jesus Christ were baptised and had the gift of the Holy Ghost given to them by authorised servants laying their hands upon their heads.

There are examples where the three-step process is demonstrated in scripture. One record is when the lead apostle, Peter, is teaching the people after they had witnessed an outpouring of the Spirit on the day of Pentecost.

'*Now when they heard this, they were pricked in their heart, and said unto Peter and to the rest of the apostles, Men and brethren, what shall we do? Then Peter said unto them, Repent, and be baptised every one of you in the name of Jesus Christ for the remission of sins, and ye shall receive the gift of the Holy Ghost.*' [Acts 2:37–38]

Here, the people saw that the kingdom of God was real when the power of the Spirit *pricked* their hearts. This was the first stage of being born-again. They were then instructed to repent, be baptised, and receive the gift of the Holy Spirit.

We learn from Acts chapter eight that the authority to bestow the gift of the Holy Spirit rested with the apostles at the time,

'*Now when the apostles which were at Jerusalem heard that Samaria had received the word of God, they sent unto them Peter and John: Who, when they were come down, prayed for them, that they might receive the Holy Ghost: (For as yet he was fallen upon none of them: only they were baptised in the name of the Lord Jesus.) Then laid they their hands on them, and they received the Holy Ghost.*' [Acts 8:14–17]

While many people were baptising, only the apostles had the authority to bestow the gift of the Holy Spirit by the laying on of hands. Philip had done the leg work in verses 12–13 to prepare the people through baptism, but he was not authorised to give the gift of the Holy Spirit. One person who was present and witnessed the additional authority of the apostles was a magician called Simon. He wanted to purchase the power with money so that whoever he laid his hands upon would also receive the gift of the Spirit. Peter utterly rebuked him and told him to repent in verses 18–22. The right to bestow this gift was not given by study, self-belief or money but by those whom God had ordained unto this power. Even the devoted missionary Philip did not pretend to have this authority.

Consider the experience of the eunuch from Ethiopia in the Book of Acts. He was the treasurer for a queen called 'Candace', so he was a trusted man in a position of authority who had come to Jerusalem to worship. His faith was not based on simply following procedure, for we find him pondering the scriptures out loud and trying to make sense of Isaiah. Most people would agree that we sometimes struggle to do the same, and he (like us) needed a little help with one of the passages. Probably due to the commotion regarding this Jesus who was crucified, the general gossip may have been centred on passages describing how the Lord would manifest himself in the flesh. Philip ran to the eunuch and asked if he understood what he was reading. The eunuch invited him up onto his carriage, where Philip taught him that the phrase,

'*He was led as a sheep to the slaughter; and like a lamb dumb before his shearer, so opened he not his mouth*' [Acts 8:32]

had reference to Jesus Christ, the Lamb of God, as taken from Isaiah 53.

Quick aside: *Interestingly, this description of the Messiah's suffering is not taught openly in synagogues today. The prescribed readings, repeated each year, do not include the verses from Isaiah 53 that would help the world see that Jesus Christ is the Messiah, just like they were supporting this* *thoughtful Ethiopian to come to the same conclusion. Christians and Jews can overlook certain scriptures, which are later clarified by the Holy Spirit when we are ready to receive them [Luke 9:45].*

Philip taught the Ethiopian many things, one of which we are led to believe is the need to be baptised. They passed by some water, and the eunuch asked if there was any reason why he should not be baptised now. He commanded that the chariot be stopped; then, he and Philip entered the water to perform the ordinance. We know from earlier in chapter eight that Philip did not have the authority to bestow the gift of the Holy Ghost by the laying on of hands, so this ordinance would be taken care of later. The eunuch went away rejoicing, having been set on the path of being born-again. No fires, gift of tongues or fanfare on this occasion. Just an honest seeker of the truth who was willing to follow the promptings of the Spirit to request baptism and enter into a commitment to follow Christ.

Jesus started his mortal work being baptised in the River Jordan by John the Baptist. He continued his work after the resurrection by appearing to his apostles and instructing them to baptise all people;

'*And Jesus came and spake unto them, saying, All power is given unto me in heaven and in earth. Go ye therefore, and teach all nations, baptising them in the name of the Father, and of the Son, and of the Holy Ghost*' [Matthew 28:18–19].

Quick aside: *The word for baptism in Greek means to 'submerge' or 'immerse'. This burial in water could represent the death and burial of our old sinful lives and the newness of life as we are born out of the water [Colossians 2:12]. A person should be old enough to decide to be baptised themselves, rather than being baptised as a baby when they don't understand their commitment.*

There is no recorded place in the New Testament where people are told they don't need to be baptised to start their journey. However, there is a place where a group of people whom John had already baptised are told that they must be baptised a second time with Jesus' baptism. Once more, we see the process of being 'born-again', which Jesus taught to Nicodemus, taking place in the lives of real people. A group who had felt the Spirit guiding them and changing their hearts had spiritually *seen* the kingdom of God but had not yet symbolically *entered* at the gate.

Paul met them,

'… *and finding certain disciples, he said unto them, Have ye received the Holy [Spirit] since ye believed? And they said unto him, We have not so much as heard whether there be any Holy [Spirit]. And he said unto them, Unto what then were ye baptised? And they said, Unto John's baptism. Then said Paul, John verily baptised with the baptism of repentance, saying unto the people, that they should believe on him which should come after him, that is, on Christ Jesus. When they heard this, they were baptised in the name of the Lord Jesus. And when Paul had laid his hands upon them, the Holy [Spirit] came on them; and they spake with tongues, and prophesied.'* [Acts 19:1–6]

Thus we witness another person with authority (in this case, Paul) initiating the physical process required for a person to be born-again. Those who had been touched by the Spirit and desired to enter into the kingdom of God were baptised (submerged or immersed) and then received the gift of the Holy Spirit through the laying on of hands by one holding the authority to do so. While this demonstrates the born-again process, it only marks the new-birth phase.

How do you know if a newborn sapling is growing up to be a fruitful man or woman in Christ? You cannot tell by listening to them shout or sing praise to the Lord, even though that is a good and joyful thing to do; you can tell by the way they love their neighbour (and their enemy) the way Jesus did.

'If ye know that he is righteous, ye know that every one that doeth righteousness is born of him.' [1 John 2:29].

To return to the beginning of the chapter and review the conversation I had with my friend, we both accepted that our arcs drawn in the sand reflected the doctrine of being born-again, but there seemed to be another glass ceiling that stopped me from entering the kingdom of heaven. He said I should accept we are 'saved by grace alone', so there was no need for me to climb the rock. He wanted me to wear the harness of grace, but suggested I could wait at the bottom of the rock for Jesus to come get me. He said that following the master climber was optional. It was a little confusing.

Chapter Five

His Graceful Harness

'At chest height, hung on the wall, is my harness'

Saved by Grace is the iconic phrase that has dominated many Christians' conversations on their journey towards the kingdom of God. The biblical use of the term 'grace' requires us to know about God's deep and abiding love for his children, which is more powerful than language has the capacity to describe.

The Greek word for 'grace' is *charis* (5485), which means favour and kindness; the Hebrew equivalent is *chen* (2580), which means favour and grace. So grace is associated with 'kindness' when transposed from Hebrew. In addition, the word 'hesed' is sometimes used.

'Hesed' or *checed* (2617) has no equivalent in English. It is sometimes translated as loving-kindness, mercy or goodness and goes back to God's covenants with Abraham, Isaac and Jacob [Micah 7:20; Isaiah 54:10]. The kind of love encapsulated by 'hesed' is like the bond between a husband and wife or a parent towards a child. When we combine the abiding covenant of a wedding vow with the love of children born into that wedding covenant, we begin to see grace's unique qualities, especially when a child chooses to go astray, as was the case with the prodigal son. Grace is the powerful covenantal love extended to all who strive to keep his commandments for a thousand generations [Deuteronomy 7:9], instantly encapsulating the repentant when they return.

To understand the richness and depth of grace, consider the many different translations of Deuteronomy 7:9. Along with *grace* (taken from the Peshitta Aramaic Bible) other translations use the words *kindness, loving-kindness, steadfast loving-kindness, steadfast love, unfailing love, mercy, loyalty, loving devotion, constant love* and *faithfulness*. These are all words used to try and pin down the powerful covenantal love that God has for his children. Each translation offers a unique perspective, adding layers of meaning to the concept.

Parental Grace

'And the child grew, and waxed strong in spirit, filled with wisdom: and the grace of God was upon him.' [Luke 2:40]

Consider the many parents who love their children and have provided all they need during their upbringing. Those children would have been protected, nourished, clothed, and educated. Moreover, they would have been loved and felt that love. Parents are powerful compared to their children. If they choose to be unloving or unkind, the child will suffer, fail to thrive, and perhaps even die. Every aspect of a parent's love for a child would come under the umbrella of 'grace', as the more powerful parent supports their weaker and dependent child. This all-pervasive principle permeates every part of a child's life and helps shape their future. While charity is the motivating feeling of love that governs our actions towards our neighbours, grace is the greater paternal love that governs God's work for his children.

Favour

Jesus was always infinitely loved by his Father, just as we are always loved the same, but his Fathers favour was something that increased [Luke 2:52]. Jesus grew into the fullness of his Father through his faithful obedience,

'*Though he were a Son, yet learned he obedience by the things which he suffered*' [Hebrews 5:8-9]

and we grow in the same way.

'*And of his fulness have all we received, and grace for grace*' [John 1:16]

As previously mentioned, the standard Hebrew and Greek definitions of *grace* include the word 'favour', in front of which some poetically add the word 'undeserved'. However, no such Greek word is in the original text. Grace is associated with favour in the same way we refer to the birthright, where the eldest child inherits a double portion of their father's kingdom and (usually) the right to rule over the house. Joseph was given a coat of many colours to symbolise the birthright which fell to him after his brother's transgression [Genesis 35:22; 49:3-4]. He grew stronger through afflictions and increased in favour with God and man [Acts 7:9-10]. This favoured position as an inheritor of the birthright is an example of the grace received by those who follow Jesus and are promised to become 'joint heirs' with him [Romans 8:17], even though they may suffer in this life. The favoured birthright can be sold and/or lost [Genesis 25:30-34; 26:1-6; 27:35-36; 1 Chronicles 5:1-2].

Rather than being 'undeserved' favour (which the NLT and CEV have a habit of inserting), the scriptures teach one must honour their covenant with God to serve him in small ways, such as feeding the hungry, clothing the naked and visiting the sick [Matthew 25:34-40]. Perhaps the NLT and CEV confuse underserved favour with underserved love. Underserved love is what every child receives in their early years, as they cannot eat, drink or keep warm without the intervention of a mother who loves them. There is no expectation of obedience on the baby's part. The same is true when we receive undeserved love and forgiveness from God at the time we are born again [Ephesians 2:8-10]. However, Jesus makes the distinction between love and favour at the end of Matthew 18 when he tells us that forgiveness can be removed but joyfully teaches it can be restored in Luke 15.

Love is forever present, but favour is not. Far from implying that we can remain in our infancy and constantly receive milk, we are taught to wholeheartedly 'put on Christ' and mature in his gospel—just as Joseph symbolically put on the coat and received real trials in his life which helped him to grow [Galatians 3:27; Ephesians 4:13-15; 1 Corinthians 13:11]. We are no longer babes who suck milk [Hebrews 5:13-14; 1 Corinthians 3:1-3], but men and women who strive to inherit the kingdom, in joint favour with Christ.

Jesus specifically told the Jews who thought they were elected through 'undeserved favour' as children of Abraham that if they were the children of Abraham, they would do the works of Abraham [John 8:37-39]. Hence, the 'election of grace'—which the NLT erroneously translates as 'undeserved kindness' in Romans 11:5—requires a person to demonstrate that they honour their Father by doing the works of faith which Abraham did, and we are required to do [Galatians 3:6-9+29]. We must emulate the works of Jesus as best we can, just as Jesus did the works of his Father [John 5:17-30; 14:21-23]. When we fail, Jesus' merciful grace will strengthen us as we try again, just like when we learned to ride a bike.

The Harness

As a parent, even though I strive to show charity to my neighbour, my children will naturally receive the next level of love, emulating God's grace. This highest level of charity is no longer restrained to loving a person as themselves but puts the needs of others above their own, such that a person would lay down their life for another. '*Greater love hath no man than this, that a man lay down his life for his friends*' [John 15:13]. So it is with grace.

My role as a parent has never been to raise my children so that, when they reach adulthood, they do not know how to look after themselves and depend on me for every little thing. I would be a poor parent if my children loved me but could not tie their shoelaces. Hopefully, the gift I have given them is all the love, skills, experiences, and financial support they will need to help them stand on their own two feet and raise a righteous posterity of their own. God's parenting goals are similar since he wants us to become 'joint heirs' with his Son [Matthew 10:24-25].

It is through the grace of God that obstacles such as physical death and sin, which block our progress, are removed. None of us could return to live in his presence without the sacrifice of Jesus Christ. Every barrier to our eternal progress has been eliminated through his name. While Abraham, Isaac, Jacob, Adam, Noah, and Moses, even down to John the Baptist, were all instruments in the hands of God, none of them could have saved us. All the sacrificial lambs offered in the temple would never bring a person back into the presence of God. The only name that can bring salvation to mankind is Jesus Christ.

When children leave their stroller pram and begin to walk outside for the first time, they are often placed into a harness so their parent can catch them if they fall. When climbing a rock face, climbers also wear a harness. The protection a harness brings symbolises the grace of our Saviour, Jesus Christ. The harness protects us as we fall but does not climb the cliff on our behalf. Without the harness, we are a fallen people, but without the wall to climb, we are no closer to the heavenly city. Just as Peter was the rock upon which the church was built [Matthew 16:18], so Christ is the rock upon which the kingdom of heaven is built [Matthew 7:24], and there is no elevator ride to the top. Once we have learned to put on the harness of grace, we must begin our climb with our loving Father watching out for us, to catch us if we fall.

The harness works when we attach ourselves to the rope by striving to keep our covenants with God. The rope marks the path or way Jesus climbed, including his atonement. The harness of grace attaches to the rope through the covenantal clip, which will be discussed more thoroughly in the next book.

The Harness of Grace is given to all who confess with their mouths that Jesus is Lord, and believe in their hearts that God raised him from the dead. We must then clip the harness to his rope which shows us the way. When we put on the harness of grace, we are choosing to put on Christ [Galatians 3:27].

After we put on the Harness

I may struggle personally to hold up Justin Bieber as an example of true doctrine, but I must nevertheless repeat the words he gave in an interview with Apple Music's Zane Lowe. He said: 'I'm not trying to earn God's love by doing good things. God has already loved me for who I am before I did anything to earn it and deserve it.' This statement is undoubtedly true and must be remembered in our discussions about grace. Whether we follow him or not, his love is unconditional and, therefore, not tied to our choosing his way of life.

The parable of the prodigal son and other parables in Luke 15 reassures us that we are always loved no matter what our sins may be.

However, Jesus did not say we can ignore his teachings, as being saved from the fall is not the same as being saved in the Kingdom. Our cannon teaches at least 40 entry requirements, which we are instructed to clip our harness of grace onto. In addition to catching us when we fall, the harness gives us extra strength to help us climb, like an exoskeleton, doubling our climbing talents.

Note: The 40 Kingdom requirements are found at the end of Part II.

The Redundant Law

Discussions about grace seem to gravitate towards 'the law' being made redundant by Jesus, replaced by his grace, but what people mean by 'the law' has changed over time [Romans 6:14]. When scripture speaks of grace, an activation mechanism of faith is also involved.

'*... but who also walk in the steps of that faith of our father Abraham... For the promise, that he should be the heir of the world, was not to Abraham, or to his seed, through* ***the law****, but through the* ***righteousness of faith****.*' [Romans 4:12–16]

Abraham walked after the 'righteousness of faith' and not after 'the law', but what was the redundant law that Paul was referring to? In the next chapter, we will look at the difference between the **law of Moses** and the **righteousness of faith**.

Chapter Six

The Bouldering Wall

*'Hearing others, I turn to see the *bouldering wall behind ... It was a training ground for the place I now stood'*

*A climbing wall used for training that does not have ropes or harnesses, as it is not very high, with mats at the bottom.

An older teenager stayed home while his parents went away for a few days. The young man called his mum to ask what was for dinner. 'Did you not see the note I left for you on the kitchen table?' asked his mum. 'Your roast dinner is in the fridge.'

I am guilty of not checking the diary or reading instructions, which has got me in trouble with my wife a few times. God also gave us several instructions, but getting on with life without checking is often easier. What if there was more to Christianity than attending church or saying you believe?

I sometimes suffer from 'man eyes' when my wife tells me to get something, but I can't see it. Her response is to walk up to the item, roll her eyes in disbelief, and ask, 'Are you blind?' God seems to have reference to this error of man as follows:

'*But in vain they do worship me, teaching for doctrines the commandments of men... Let them alone: they be blind leaders of the blind. And if the blind lead the blind, both shall fall into the ditch*' [Matthew 15:9,14].

In this chapter, we look at the principle of 'works' and how it became one of the commandments of men, where well-meaning teachers accidentally lead followers astray due to a semantic change over time rather than a purposeful piracy of Christ's doctrines. Paul often said we could not be saved by works, but was he referring to the works of the law of Moses or the law of righteousness that Jesus taught? Understanding this doctrine requires some historical background in Paul's writings, as many of his epistles (letters) are concerned with instructing Jewish converts who wanted to keep the law of Moses.

'*Knowing that a man is not justified by the works of the law, but by the faith of Jesus Christ, even we have believed in Jesus Christ, that we might be justified by the faith of Christ, and not by the works of the law: for by the works of the law shall no flesh be justified.*' [Galatians 2:16]

The 'law of Moses' was given to the children of Israel after Jehovah had already given them the Ten Commandments from Mount Sinai. He spoke the commandments amidst thundering and lightning with trumpets and smoke, but the people quickly broke them, so the law of Moses resulted from their disobedience. It was a law of 613 strict rules and regulations encompassing the 'law of performances and ordinances', which included circumcision. Still, it was abbreviated to become known as the 'law of works' and was designed to point people towards the Messiah, who would eventually come to save the world from sin.

The people in Jesus' day had been schooled all their lives in the law of Moses, yet did not understand it, or they would have accepted Jesus Christ as their Messiah [John 5:46–47]. They knew they needed a Saviour but were looking for a military leader to deliver them from the Romans, not realising he was to be their sacrificial lamb to save them from their sins.

We will look at how some early converts to Christianity wanted to continue keeping the law of works (Moses), even though it was now fulfilled in Christ. The contention from disagreements on how to apply the law of circumcision etc. to the new Christian faith was so significant that it led to Paul writing extensively on the subject. In the book of Acts, chapter fifteen, the backlash from those who wanted to continue keeping the law came to a head.

'*And certain men which came down from Judæa taught the brethren, and said, Except ye be circumcised after the manner of Moses, ye cannot be saved ... And the apostles and elders came together [to consider] this matter.*' [Acts 15:1–6]

The question of whether they should continue to keep the law of Moses was a difficult one. It had not yet been officially resolved, even among the apostles. They held a special meeting to address the concern, the result of which was to declare that the law (including circumcision) was now obsolete. Their decision was communicated to the church as follows:

'*And they wrote letters by them after this manner; ... Forasmuch as we have heard, that certain which went out from us have troubled you with words, subverting your souls, saying, Ye must be circumcised, and keep the law: to whom we gave no such commandment: ... For it seemed good to the Holy [Spirit], and to us, to lay upon you no greater burden than these necessary things; ... That ye abstain from meats offered to idols, and from blood, and from things strangled, and from fornication: from which if ye keep yourselves, ye shall do well.*' [Acts 15:23–29]

So, under inspiration, the apostles ended the practice of the law of Moses, except for the few items listed above. We should give the new converts some slack because even the apostles were still getting to grips with the fulfilment of the law and the new covenant (New Testament). The change was significant news. It was the equivalent of Jesus coming tomorrow and ending the practice of taking bread and wine. Imagine if he did that!

The law of Moses was replaced by the law of faith in Christ, who is the Alpha & Omega (beginning and end) of our faith. When we follow the teachings of Jesus, which is his law, we are acting in faith. The law of Christ is referred to as the law of faith, or simply faith. Indeed, Paul often refers to the laws of Moses and of Circumcision as 'works' and the law of Jesus as 'faith'.

It's crucial to grasp the monumental shift in a Jewish converts mind-set necessary to move on from the law of Moses. Paul confronts this head-on in his epistle to the Romans.

'*Then what advantage has the Jew? Or what is the value of circumcision? ... What then? Are we Jews any better off? No, not at all ... Now we know that whatever the law says it speaks to those who are under the law ... For by works of the law no human being will be justified in his sight.*' [Romans 3:1–20 ESV shortened]

Paul continues:

'Then what becomes of our boasting? It is excluded. By what kind of law? By a law of works? No, but by the law of faith. For we hold the one is justified by faith apart from works of the law.' [Romans 3:27–29 ESV]

He sounds exasperated as he tries to help change the thinking of Jewish Christians. The 'works' contained in the performances and ordinances of the Law of Moses—which only the Jews performed—were now obsolete; they were replaced by the law of faith, which is also referred to as the law of righteousness.

One of my retired work colleagues is an active minister and has been energetic in proclaiming that the scriptures teach we no longer need to follow Jesus' commandments to receive salvation. He firmly believes in this teaching, and his joy and love for the Lord are self-evident. We have spent many hours discussing the gospel and found much common ground. However, the community he belongs to has built an entire faith system based around shunning personal commitments and placed all effort at the feet of Jesus, with no responsibility to follow him. Their faith system embraced the semantic change of the word 'works' from Paul's teachings of the 'law of Moses' to now refer to not keeping any of the commandments at all. This semantic transition has become a significant stumbling block on the Christian road back home. Just as some Israelites may have stumbled by thinking they could be saved by keeping the law of Moses alone, some Christians are now taught that they can continue to be saved without keeping any of God's commandments at all.

'But Israel, which followed after the law of righteousness, hath not attained to the law of righteousness. Wherefore? Because they sought it not by faith, but as it were by the works of the law. For they stumbled at that stumblingstone' [Romans 9:31–32].

Let us not stumble by believing the works of Moses and the works of faith are the same. Paul never excuses Christians from keeping the commandments but tells all Christians to keep them and put on the armour of light! [Romans 13].

Most conversations I have had with fellow Christians end up agreeing that while we cannot be saved without grace, we cannot continue to be saved without striving to love our neighbours as ourselves. Some say that a person wasn't saved in the first place if they don't then naturally follow Jesus, intrinsically inferring there must be a measure of change in the character of the person saved. This change includes striving to keep the commandments and repenting daily when we fall short. Despite many rocky beginnings to such conversations, we understand each other and realise we are coming to the same truth from two different viewpoints, just like the two arcs drawn upside down that form the sign of a fish. The harness of his grace saves us if we fall, but if we fail to keep climbing, grace alone will not winch us up for free.

Performing miracles in the name of Jesus is not a sign of personal righteousness.

'*Many will say to me in that day, Lord, Lord, have we not prophesied in thy name? and in thy name have cast out devils? and in thy name done many wonderful works? And then will I profess unto them, I never knew you: depart from me, ye that work iniquity.*' [Matthew 7:22–23]

We are counselled to get to know God to receive eternal life.

'*And this is life eternal, that they might know thee the only true God, and Jesus Christ, whom thou hast sent*' [John 17:3]

We get to know him by keeping his commandments.

'*And hereby we do know that we know him, if we keep his commandments. He that saith, I know him, and keepeth not his commandments, is a liar, and the truth is not in him*' [1 John 2:1–5].

The Ten Commandments

We have seen that the law of performances and ordinances contained in the law of Moses would become obsolete, but where does that leave the Ten Commandments? Were they included in the law of Moses? First, some history for context.

After the life of Joseph (coat of many colours) played out, and the children of Israel had been in Egypt for about 400 years, they became slaves of the new Pharaoh. Long story short, they were led to freedom by Moses and received their symbolic baptism as they crossed the Red Sea on dry ground. The destruction of the Egyptian army followed, and the children of Israel were now free for the first time in generations. During their captivity, some or all of their traditional forms of worship had become corrupt through mingling their Abrahamic religion with the Egyptian belief system. As revealed to them in the past through Abraham, Isaac, and Jacob, the law of Righteousness had become polluted and diluted. Moses tried to actively reinstitute the laws of sacrifice and judgments among the people of Israel before they arrived at Mount Sinai.

Upon their arrival, the voice of the Lord (Jehovah) was heard giving them the Ten Commandments, as famously recorded in Exodus 20. They all agreed with one voice that they would keep them [Exodus 24:3–7], and in chapter 31, Moses was given the commandments written on stone by the finger of God [31:18]. Still, when he descended from the mount, the people were found worshipping idols in direct contradiction to the second commandment. Moses breaks the stone tablets written by the finger of the Lord [chapter 32], and the Tabernacle is moved far away from the camp [33:7], symbolising God's displeasure with the people.

Moses made new stone tablets, which he carried up the mount and wrote upon them the words of the covenant, the ten commandments [Exodus 34:27-28; Deuteronomy 10:1-2].

It is important to note that these stone tablets were placed inside the Arc of the Covenant [Deuteronomy 10:2+5], which Indiana Jones made famous.

The Lord later spoke to Moses out of the Tabernacle and revealed the 'Law of Works', which takes up almost the whole book of Leviticus! This law of works was added because they transgressed the original covenant [Galatians 3:19]. It was in addition to the Ten Commandments and given much later after the Tabernacle had been constructed.

So, Jehovah revealed the Ten Commandments from Mount Sinai, wrote them on stone, and had them placed inside the Ark of the Covenant. Afterwards, the law of works was written by Moses on gevil (cow-hide) and kept on the outside of the Ark (the Hebrew word for 'beside' is used) [Deuteronomy 31:24–26]. Thus, we see the Ten Commandments were not referred to by Paul, the apostle when he pleaded with the people not to rely on the old 'works' of the law, for they were written at different times, on different materials and placed in separate locations.

Quick aside: *The Ten Commandments were exemplified by Jesus before his death and taught by the apostles after his resurrection. The following table compares the commandments in Exodus 20 with the teachings of Jesus and his apostles.*

Commandment	By Jesus	By Apostles
1	Matthew 4:10	Acts 14:11-15
2	Mark 12:14-17	Acts 15:20
3	Matthew 5:33-37	James 5:12
4	Mark 2:28	Acts 18:4
5	Matthew 15:3-8	Ephesians 6:1-2
6	Matthew 19:17-19	Romans 13:8-10
7	Matthew 19:17-19	Romans 13:8-10
8	Matthew 19:17-19	Romans 13:8-10
9	Matthew 19:17-19	Romans 13:8-10
10	Matthew 6:19-21	Romans 13:8-10
Note: The commandments are independent in their sphere, with no regard to nation or dispensation. The author's website provides information on the philosophy of *dispensationalism*.		

Paul mostly speaks about the law of works pertaining to the Mosaic law, but other canonical authors refer to works in a more contemporary fashion. James is the most famous scriptural author to address the non-Mosaic subject of works.

'*But be ye doers of the word, and not hearers only, deceiving your own selves.*' [James1:22]

'*Even so, faith, if it hath not works, is dead, being alone. Yea, a man may say, Thou hast faith, and I have works: shew me thy faith without thy works, and I will shew thee my faith by my works ... But wilt thou know, O vain man, that faith without works is dead?*' [James 2:17–20]

In the middle of these passages is the damning and almost sarcastic observation:

'Thou believest that there is one God; thou doest well: the devils also believe, and tremble' [V.19].

There are accounts in the New Testament where devils are heard to testify that Jesus is the very Christ, and they certainly believe it. Still, nobody would pass salvation onto a devil simply because they confess Jesus' name. So, we, too, cannot expect salvation by confession alone. Confession is just one of the entry requirements.

University Work

The 'bouldering wall' mentioned in the parable of the clip represented the primary school of Moses, or the law of works, where there was learning but no specific qualifications. Moses was the schoolmaster back then. Now, the rock facing each of us is our final stage of education, our university of life, where the results are crucial enough to determine our eternal destination. The tuition and accommodation fees are so unaffordable that no person can pay them, so our loving Father has gracefully paid them for us [Matthew 18:23-27]. Now we are here, and he has sent lecturers and professors to teach us how to pass our exams, but the teachers can only show us the way, not do the work for us. We must grow like a seed, learn from our mistakes, and compile evidence to support our learning. We must demonstrate that we understand each subject and can apply the laws we have been taught. This learning is only possible because Jesus pays our fee.

If a university gave all students a pass with no growth on their part, there would be little point in going there. The student's time would have been wasted as nobody on earth or in heaven would take their qualification seriously. It would be a worthless degree. The University of Life is designed to mould and shape us to become ready to inherit the family business and become joint heirs with the Son [Romans 8:17; Luke 15:11-31]. Our Father sponsors us and has given us everything we need to succeed spiritually. We must listen to the professors, work smartly, and provide evidence supporting our type of celestial graduation (see 1 Corinthians 15:41-42). While today we are Padawans of the Master, we will one day have completed our training and be presented before the heavenly council to be judged according to the evidence inside our characters.

***Quick aside**: I was often perplexed when reading the parable of the Prodigal Son in Luke 15. We can understand the loving embrace of a forgiving father, who saw his son far off and ran to him, but the part about the begrudging brother was troubling to me. How does he fit into the parable of heaven? The father said to him, 'All that is mine is yours', which sounds like he was saying the prodigal son (who was forgiven) would have no further hope of inheritance, as the brother now has it all. How could this be a correct teaching of heaven? Do the repentant children have no hope of reward? One day, I saw the answer in my mind's eye, and suddenly, the whole thing made sense. Of course, we can substitute ourselves for the prodigal son, but what happens when we substitute Jesus for the faithful brother?*

Jesus would have rejoiced with his Father over the brother who returned [Hebrews 2:17-18]. The Father would rightly say to the sinless Jesus, 'All that is mine is yours', but the difference is Jesus would turn to the brother and say, 'Come follow me, and I will make you a joint-heir' [Romans 8:17].

The judgment seat must determine if we are ready to represent the Father as kings and priests [Revelation 1:5-6] and inherit eternal life. I am so thankful that my tuition fees are paid, my books are supplied, and my accommodation is taken care of. Now, I must knuckle down before my course is over to show my Father that I love him and demonstrate I am willing to keep his commandments, even if I sometimes get poor grades along the way [John 14:15].

Evidence of Ergon

Suffragettes motto: deeds not words

At the Last Supper, the Lord asked his disciples who was greater in the kingdom: Was it he who sits with the food or he who serves? He then tells Simon Peter, '*When thou art converted, strengthen thy brethren*' [Luke 22:26-32]. Simon protested and tried to show through his words that he was already converted, but Jesus prophesied that, by the time the cock crowed thrice, his words would have come to nothing. People are transformed when they have turned back from old ways and converted their love for the Lord into personality traits rather than feelings. We cannot join a gym and expect to get fit by looking at the equipment. Peter showed through his life that he learned from his lessons and was undoubtedly worthy of the kingdom, even though he stumbled occasionally.

One conversation with a fellow climber brought forth much fruit on the subject of salvation by grace. As we peacefully discussed the topic in Norwich, it became apparent we were applying the same principles but determining our word choice differently. We started by discussing the words of Jesus himself.

'*Every tree that bringeth not forth good fruit is hewn down, and cast into the fire. Wherefore by their fruits ye shall know them. Not every one that saith unto me, Lord, Lord, shall enter into the kingdom of heaven; but he that doeth the will of my Father which is in heaven.*' [Matthew 7:19–21]

While he suggested we did not need to work, he did agree that we needed to show evidence of our conversion. He used an apple tree as an example, saying we cannot pretend to be someone other than who we are because our fruits define us. An apple tree does not bring forth oranges. As Christians, he said we need to demonstrate our love of Christ through the evidence in our lives. I agreed with him, as both works and evidence are the same.

The Greek words for 'works' in scripture include *ergon* and *erga*, which refer to any act of work whether it be religious or general. Words are best understood when viewed in the context of the verse to decide which application to use. The following are examples from scripture that discuss different types of 'works' mentioned in the New Testament.

God will not save us by keeping the Law of Works (i.e. **Law of Moses)**	**We are to be judged by our works**
Romans 3:20+27-28	Ecclesiastes 12:13–14
Romans 4:2-13	Matthew 7:21-23
Romans 11:5–7	Matthew 16:24-27
Galatians 2:16	Galatians 6:7
Galatians 3:2-5	Titus 1:16
Ephesians 2:7-15	1 Timothy 6:18-19
We do not work to earn forgiveness.	1 Peter 1:17+22-23
Titus 3:3-5	Hebrews 10:24-29
Ephesians 2:8-10	Revelation 2:26; Matthew 25:20-21
Romans 3:24-25	Revelation 20:12-13
Note: *Justification means forgiveness from sin.*	Revelation 22:12
	1 Corinthians 3:6-8

	Additional references
	Acts 26:19-20
	John 8:39
	2 Timothy 3:16-17
	James 1:22+2:17-20+22–24
	Hebrews 13:21; Matthew 5:48; Revelation 3:2
	Matthew 5:16

By taking the time to consider the way of salvation taught in scripture, we become more united as a group of disciples under the banner of Christ. While we all strive to be of '*one Lord, one faith, one baptism, one God*' [Ephesians 4:5–6], we each come to the table with different upbringings and backgrounds. God encouraged us to use '*reason*' to understand heavenly things.

'*Come now, and let us reason together, saith the Lord: though your sins be as scarlet, they shall be as white as snow; though they be red like crimson, they shall be as wool. If ye be willing and obedient, ye shall eat the good of the land.*' [Isaiah 1:18–19]

It is reasonable that if Jesus told us to follow in his footsteps and handgrips, we should diligently do our best, helping fellow climbers as we go. This active participation in our faith journey not only motivates us but also engages us in the community, strengthening our bonds with fellow disciples. Waiting and singing at the bottom of the cliff while wearing his graceful harness is not a reasonable way of following Jesus.

Like the teenager left at home with instructions on finding food, we might also need to look deeper or work harder to grow healthy fruit. We don't need to cook up new doctrines of fast-food salvation ourselves, as the nourishment of the gospel is there for us to enjoy. If we were to watch a reality T.V. show where a teenager was left alone with a bountiful array of food in the fridge but sat and starved at the kitchen table, we would all shout at the TV for them to open the fridge! How much worse it would be if the youth read the note on the table and said that his parents had provided the food; therefore, he did not need to eat it.

Some spiritually refuse to eat the life-changing food of the gospel, as they say, Jesus has eaten it for them. They feel they don't need the spiritual nourishment of doing good. Jesus spoke of how food and work are symbols of the same thing,

'In the mean while his disciples prayed him, saying, Master, eat. But he said unto them, I have meat to eat that ye know not of. Therefore said the disciples one to another, Hath any man brought him ought to eat? Jesus saith unto them, My meat is to do the will of him that sent me, and to finish his work.' [John 4:31–34]

Regarding feeding the 5,000 (plus women and children), Jesus said:

'Verily, verily, I say unto you, Ye seek me, not because ye saw the miracles, but because ye did eat of the loaves, and were filled. Labour not for the meat which perisheth, but for that meat which endureth unto everlasting life, which the Son of man shall give unto you.' [John 6:26–27; Matthew 14:21] i.e. he gives us teachings & commandments [John 13:34-35]

This statement about labour caused a great question in the disciple's minds, leading us into the next chapter:

'Then said they unto him, What shall we do, that we might work the works of God?' [John 6:28]

What nourishment will keep us from spiritual starvation? What is the 'labour' Jesus said we must do? Now that we have moved on from Moses' limited bouldering wall, how do we use our belief in Jesus to help us climb towards the city of Christ? There is no better place to study the things Jesus wanted us to do than in the Sermon on the Mount, the sermon that changed the world.

Chapter Seven

The Rope and the Clip

(Sermon on the Mount – Part One)

'He abseiled down to tell climbers how to use the rope ... Obediently, I opened the magenta carabineer on the harness and clipped on'

The teachings of the Saviour found in the Sermon on the Mount are (to me) the most precious and beautifully spoken doctrines in our scriptural canon. Here, we see just what the Lord came to teach his people. It combines the very best of the Old and New Testaments. Chapters five to seven of the book of Matthew are where we learn that the 'law of Moses' was to be upgraded to the 'law of Faith' once it had been fulfilled.

The Beatitudes are given at the beginning:

'Blessed are the poor in spirit: for theirs is the kingdom of heaven.
Blessed are they that mourn: for they shall be comforted.
Blessed are the meek: for they shall inherit the earth.
Blessed are they which do hunger and thirst after Righteousness: for they shall be filled.
Blessed are the merciful: for they shall obtain mercy.
Blessed are the pure in heart: for they shall see God.
Blessed are the peacemakers: for they shall be called the children of God.' [Matthew 5:3-11]

Notice how they are not new commandments on what we should do; instead, they are attitudes of the heart on how we should be. This revived law of faith encourages us to become righteous rather than just act righteously. The Latin word 'beatus' is the root from which we derive the word 'beatitudes' in English, which means to be fortunate, happy, and blessed. These are the attributes Jesus has; all those who enter heaven will have the same mindset of happiness and gratitude for their blessings.

One day, my youngest daughter returned from church and showed me a list of gifts she felt she had received in life. The teacher had asked them to list ten things they were grateful for, but she wrote down twenty-one of her blessings and why she was thankful for them. I will treasure this list, not because of her blessings but because of her attitude of gratitude. Her list was a window into her soul.

Often, I meet genuinely lovely people who may have no religion or understanding of who Jesus Christ is, yet they are still close to him through their attitude toward others. While honouring our Father by keeping his commandments is an essential goal, so are the attitudes of heart described in this sermon. A righteous person may discover Christ late in life, but their kind acts before encountering him will have helped shape them into Christ's image. A person who was baptised in their youth yet never developed these attributes will be found lacking. The Ten Commandments are the root, and the Beatitudes are the fruit. Jesus spoke clearly about the kind of person he is asking us to become through the declaration of the Beatitudes (see Paul's version in Ephesians 4:21-32).

After giving these, Jesus straight away told his followers,

'Ye are the salt of the earth: but if the salt have lost his savour, wherewith shall it be salted? it is thenceforth good for nothing, but to be cast out, and to be trodden under foot of men.' [Matthew 5:13]

The term *salt* refers to a high-value commodity with significant effects, even in small quantities. Some people of the era were rumoured to have received their wages in salt, which might be where the word 'salary' comes from, as the Latin root 'sal' means salt. Pure salt does not lose its flavour on its own, but when mixed with other compounds, it can become polluted and worthless.

A small amount can flavour a whole meal; it is a preservative, soaks up blood, and salt is a natural healer when used with skill. All of these applications carry metaphoric weight. As Christians, we are to be the small part of the world that enhances people's lives by the simple acts of kindness we do. Should we cease to be kind and loving to our neighbour, we would metaphorically be cast out on the day of judgment and '*trodden underfoot*', like the seed that fell by the wayside in the parable of the sower [Luke 8:5].

Jesus continues this train of thought in the subsequent parable by explaining,

'Ye are the light of the world. A city that is set on an hill cannot be hid. Neither do men light a candle, and put it under a bushel, but on a candlestick; and it giveth light unto all that are in the house. Let your light so shine before men, that they may see your good works, and glorify your Father which is in heaven.' [Matthew 5:14-15]

Once again, we are commanded to do good works and 'be' Christians rather than just 'believe' in Christianity. Our motivation for good works should be for God's glory due to our love for him and our fellow man, just as Jesus glorified his Father with his works [John 17:4; 20:21]. Our light will attract others to be a part of the Christian society, and the more lights that gather together, the warmer and brighter it is for everyone.

I remember being taught many years ago the reason for being active in a church community. A friend visited an older man on a cold winter's evening. As they sat around a warm fire together, the friend asked why he should bother attending church each week, as he could be a good person on his own without the need for organised religion. The older man took a coal from the bucket and placed it on the fire. They watched the coal glow red hot in the company of other coals and give off heat and light of its own. The man then took the coal off the fire and set it to the side of the pit. Slowly, the coal lost its glow and died without any nearby heat to keep it going. The man thanked his old friend for the lesson, and together, they talked into the night about the people who had lit up their lives and warmed their souls.

Parents, pastors, friends, and associates all have a contribution to make, and you may feel that your little coal will not give out much heat at all. Perhaps you are right, but your light may be just enough to keep the flame in someone else's life alive, and, without knowing it, you have helped to save a soul whom you never knew [Matthew 25:34-40]. We 'glow' to church so that others can feel our warmth.

Conversely, church activity can be likened to a family going on holiday who arrive at the airport with their hand luggage and check-in. They go to the gate and hear the call for their flight to depart but ignore it. They sit looking out at the aircraft and enjoy the food in the lounge. They try to catch some sleep on the uncomfortable pews and enjoy their day-long vacation. Ultimately, they go home. What a waste! So it is that some turn up to church, thinking that church is the final destination. Looking past opportunities for service, to become an angel to someone else, they miss the point of worship and return home without ever understanding what the brochure was talking about. The chapel is just the departure lounge for a sermon that should last all week and bring joyful memories.

The churches we belong to are not sanctuaries for the sanctified but service stations for the community and individuals who attend. Our friends, families, and fellow citizens on the journey are kept warm and spiritually nourished by the company of the membership. Small daily service candles are more worthwhile than a grand bonfire of service once a year. The parable of the widow's mite reminds us that even our most minor acts of kindness will be held in high esteem, whether face-to-face service or genuine compassion over virtual platforms in times of isolation. It is the thought, followed by an action, that counts.

Next up, in the Sermon on the Mount, Jesus tells us,

'Do not think that I have come to abolish the Law or the Prophets; I have not come to abolish them but to fulfil them' [ESV v.17].

The law of animal sacrifice was to be fulfilled by Jesus, but the principles upon which it was founded were not abolished, or else there would be no need for the sacrifice in the first place. Jesus took upon himself the sins of the world, such that he became the living sacrifice for us today. Through his death, he rent the veil in the temple, negating the need for the high priests to offer animal sacrifices on our behalf.

'For such an high priest became us, who is holy, harmless, undefiled, separate from sinners, and made higher than the heavens; Who needeth not daily, as those high priests, to offer up sacrifice, first for his own sins, and then for the people's: for this he did once, when he offered up himself.' [Hebrews 7:27; 2:17]

We no longer needed to sacrifice animals on an altar, but the law of sacrifice was still active through Jesus. He was now the mediator for our sins rather than the Levite priests [Hebrews 7:11–12]. Hence, the law was upheld and fulfilled rather than abolished. We can imagine that keeping the law of Moses was equivalent to learning to drive in an instructor's car. When Jesus came along, he did not tell us to stop learning to drive; instead, he gracefully bought us a car and became our examiner, thus fulfilling the law and not destroying it. In addition, he has set out the terms of our insurance, which gift is called repentance and is given to those of a broken car and a contrite spirit.

If a child has an accident and crashes the family car, they may well be in fear of the wrath of their dad when he discovers their mistake. In contrast, as soon as we hang our heads in sadness for our sins, our Heavenly Father rejoices that we have felt the need to improve our lives and hugs us. No person's life is so much of a car crash that they cannot humbly take the wreck of their lives to the Father, who then shows us to the garage of Christ. He has fulfilled the law of sacrifice and is now our great Mechanical High Priest.

When Jesus suffered in Gethsemane and on the cross, he may have had your life pass across his spiritual view. He may have felt the agonies of your heart while spiritually alongside you in your time of need. He is there by our side when we suffer, waiting for us to turn to him and place our burdens at his feet. Please turn to him and receive the light of his love, which melts our souls and moulds us into new people.

When we did not cause the car crash, he can equally take away the pain and fix our lives so we can walk fresh and new with him. He suffered for all our pain, not just our mistakes, so we can ask for healing from the wicked acts of others. He is the only one who truly knows how we feel;

he felt it with us in Gethsemane and on the cross. With his help, the things we suffer and endure become oil in our lamps so we can, too, be a light to others, as he asks us to be.

Next, in the sermon, Jesus tells us that whoever keeps the commandments will be called 'great' in the kingdom of heaven and goes on to enhance them.

Enhancing the Ten

The Ten Commandments are a part of the law of faith, not the law of Moses, and were expanded upon by Jesus in the Sermon on the Mount. The following is an example of how the people were to enhance their obedience rather than lay their observation aside.

'Ye have heard that it was said by them of old time, Thou shalt not kill; and whosoever shall kill shall be in danger of the judgment: But I say unto you, That whosoever is angry with his brother ... shall be in danger of the judgment: and whosoever shall say to his brother, Raca, shall be in danger of the council: but whosoever shall say, Thou fool, shall be in danger of hell fire.' [Matthew 5:21-22]

This example illustrates how the spirit of the law is more encapsulating than the letter of it. While a person may justify their sins because they are not expressly forbidden in the written word, Jesus shone the light of wisdom on the pathway of those who walk by faith. Rather than replacing the Ten Commandments, Jesus helped us to live them to their fullness.

By expounding the commandments, we gain insight into how the people lived under the law of righteousness that Abraham taught his children. Before the Ten Commandments were written in stone, the people of God lived with commandments in the '*fleshy tables of the heart*', a concept that Paul expected the early saints to embody [2 Corinthians 3:2-3; Proverbs 3:3-4].

The law of sacrifice—pointing to Jesus Christ—was around long before Moses. The law of Righteousness that Abraham lived under would have been kept by the children of Israel if they hadn't slid back to worshipping idols so quickly after Moses went up the mountain.

'*This is what I mean: the law, which came 430 years afterward, does not annul a covenant previously ratified by God, so as to make the promise void ... Why then the law? It was added because of transgressions, until the offspring should come to whom the promise had been made*' [Galatians 3:17–19 ESV]

If Israel had kept the whole law of Moses in faith, they would have also kept the Ten Commandments and lived in Righteousness under the law of Righteousness, but they could not see past the law to its intended meaning, so they stumbled. They kept the law of works but ignored the law of Righteousness, which comes by faith or faithful living.

'*But Israel, which followed after the law of Righteousness, hath not attained to the law of Righteousness. Wherefore? Because they sought it not by faith, but as it were by the works of the law. For they stumbled at that stumblingstone.'* [Romans 9:31–32]

Living by our faith in Christ means we have graduated from primary school and are trusted to keep the law of Righteousness without the strictness of the law of Moses. How saddening it would be for God if we slid back into sin, just as the children of Israel slid back when Moses went up the mountain. We would be no better than they were. We need to be Christlike in heaven by serving God [Revelation 22:3], so now is our chance to practice on Earth by serving our fellow man. Hence, there is a need to practice keeping the commandments in mortality, such that faithfulness to the laws of heaven becomes second nature to us and forms the very fabric of our souls, just as Abraham walked in faith [Romans 4:12–13]. An old saying goes, 'Practice makes Perfect', but in our case, our practice is enhanced by the grace of Jesus Christ who strengthens us, and helps us to become perfect, as he charged us to do in Matthew 5:48.

Quick aside: *The Righteousness spoken of which comes through faith was not unique to Abraham. Noah was the heir of Righteousness, which means the righteousness of faith was taught and practised even before his time [Hebrews 11:7]. It is reasonable to assume that all the prophets, back to Adam, taught their children the 'Righteousness of Faith'. Righteousness means 'right judgments' and is the sum of what our Father hopes his children will demonstrate while here on earth. Right judgments are always rooted in love for our fellow man [Genesis 18:18–19].*

The Ten Commandments were a measuring stick given to the children of Israel upon which they could build a righteous life and judge correctly rather than a complete list of do's and don'ts. Seeing the people were not living up to these principles, Jesus gave the sermon on the Mount to expound the commandments and exhort them to live more faithfully, which they should have been doing from the time of Sinai, and even beforehand in Egypt.

Stepping back a moment, Jesus ensured that nobody took the coming of the Messiah as a release from keeping God's commandments.

'*Whosoever therefore shall break one of these least commandments, and shall teach men so, he shall be called the least in the kingdom of heaven.*' [Matthew 5:19; 1 John 2:4]

This statement leads naturally to his council against the local leaders and teachers of his time:

'*… unless your Righteousness exceeds that of the scribes and Pharisees, you will never enter the kingdom of heaven.*' [Matthew 5:20 ESV]

Remember that Nicodemus was a Pharisee to whom Jesus revealed the principle of being born-again. Here, Jesus places the act of entering the kingdom of heaven in association with keeping the commandments and should rightly be considered **'Step Four'** in the born-again process. While the opposition focused on massaging their egos on the public stage, Jesus wanted something more holy and heart-centred from us. Becoming a 'Christian-

Pharisee' is possible by strictly adhering to some aspects of the gospel and ignoring others. As Jesus said, '*These ought ye to have done, and not to leave the other undone.*' [Matthew 23:23]

From Matthew 5:21 to 7:27, Christ's teachings enhance the commandments, not by replacing them but by building them up. Christ teaches how our attitudes should be toward the commandments and, more specifically, our fellow man. We will pick up the Sermon from Matthew 7:12, but a thorough, prayerful study of the whole Sermon will lead us through the entry gate of heaven. Jesus is the best teacher, and we sit at his feet when reading Matthew 5–7.

The Golden Rule (from the sermon)

'Therefore all things whatsoever ye would that men should do to you, do ye even so to them: for this is the law and the prophets.' [Matthew 7:12]

How many faithful mothers and fathers have counselled their children throughout time with this priceless saying of Jesus? The other example of the '*law and the prophets*' being explained in such a simple phrase is when a Pharisee lawyer asked Jesus, *'Master, what is the great commandment in the law?'* Jesus replied using the Old Testament as his guide,

'Thou shalt love the Lord thy God with all thy heart, and with all thy soul, and with all thy mind. This is the first and great commandment. And the second is like unto it, Thou shalt love thy neighbour as thyself. On these two

commandments hang all the law and the prophets' [Matthew 22:36–40].

These two great commandments were not new. The first part encapsulates the first four of the Ten Commandments and was initially found in Deuteronomy:

'*And thou shalt love the Lord thy God with all thine heart, and with all thy soul, and with all thy might*' [Deuteronomy 6:5].

The second part covers commandments five to ten and echoes the book of Leviticus,

'*... but thou shalt love thy neighbour as thyself: I am the Lord*' [Leviticus 19:18].

If we were to keep the two great commandments, the other ten would naturally fall into place as they are just practical examples of the first two. We could even make up our own personal commandments, such as: 'I will not gossip' or 'I will always use kind words' as these things are similar to the other commandments and extrapolated from the principles in the two great ones. Commandments should serve to lift us up to higher and holier habits.

The golden rule was actively taught among the Jews at the time of Jesus as the lead-up question to the parable of the Good Samaritan outlines:

'And, behold, a certain lawyer stood up, and tempted him, saying, Master, what shall I do to inherit eternal life? He said unto him, What is written in the law? how readest

thou? And he answering said, Thou shalt love the Lord thy God with all thy heart, and with all thy soul, and with all thy strength, and with all thy mind; and thy neighbour as thyself. And he said unto him, Thou hast answered right: this do, and thou shalt live.' [Luke 10:25–28]

Jesus then proceeds to teach the parable of the *Good Samaritan*, which is the embodiment of the Golden Rule.

The closer we come to living as the Saviour taught, the less we need the commandments to tell us what to do and the more we rely on the spirit in which the commandments were given. When we follow these principles, our works will become the works of Christ, and, on Judgment Day, we will meet our friend and co-worker with whom we will have shared a yoke [Matthew 11:28–30]. To sum up the law of faith practically, we can refer to the book of James. He describes the actions of faith as '*the perfect law of liberty*' and '*pure religion*', to which sentiment I could not agree more:

'But whoso looketh into the perfect law of liberty, and continueth therein, he being not a forgetful hearer, but a doer of the work, this man shall be blessed in his deed ... Pure religion and undefiled before God and the Father is this, To visit the fatherless and widows in their affliction, and to keep himself unspotted from the world.' [James 1:25–27]

The reason it is called the perfect law of liberty is that a person who follows the fruits of the spirit in this way will not be violating any law and, hence, will be living as Jesus did throughout his life, not subject to any punishment,

'*But the fruit of the Spirit is love, joy, peace, longsuffering, gentleness, goodness, faith, meekness, temperance: against such there is no law.*' [Galatians 5:22-23]

The point of all the commandments is to help us become the kind of people who do not need any commandments, for in heaven, we must be perfect. Perfection is not a gift but an end goal. Jesus wants all of us to be even as his Father is,

'*You therefore must be perfect, as your heavenly Father is perfect.*' [ESV Matthew 5:48].

The law of Righteousness, simply put, is the law of loving God and our fellow man. Once we have mastered these, we can discard the rules, like when we learned to ride a bike and discarded the stabilisers. We believe and then work to become a well-balanced Christian.

Years ago, when a person was being trained in a new career, teaching them how to do the job was called 'showing them the rope(s)', a nautical idiom. When Jesus taught us his perfect example of how to 'be' in the Sermon on the Mount, he 'showed us the rope'. As the lead climber on our expedition of life, we are safe when we attach ourselves to his teachings. We are to follow his two great commandments, behind which all others fall into place. At the time of the Sermon on the Mount, many listeners clipped onto his teachings with great zeal, only to unclip themselves later and fall away.

Chapter Eight

Fellow Climbers

(Sermon on the Mount – Part Two)

'A number of us stand at the wall with stories and advice for each other'

My talented wife is a keen gardener and takes joy in her harvest. One particular stress each year is the pesky squirrel that comes close to the house and steals her hazelnuts just before they are ready to eat. She keeps watch each day and monitors their growth. The yield is low, yet her joy is complete when she triumphantly beats the squirrel!

Jesus knew he would be taken from his sheep one day, and the remaining shepherds would be left to guide his flock on earth without him physically being there to lead them. As we approach the end of the Sermon on the Mount, our Chief Shepherd instructs his followers how to trust a person to be their teacher after he has gone.

'Beware of false prophets, which come to you in sheep's clothing, but inwardly they are ravening wolves. Ye shall know them by their fruits. Do men gather grapes of thorns, or figs of thistles? ... Every tree that bringeth not forth good fruit is hewn down and cast into the fire. Wherefore by their fruits, ye shall know them.' [Matthew 7:15–20]

Jesus loves all his sheep throughout all generations, so he is anxious for them not to be deceived. Here, in the Sermon, he gives us a key of judgment to discern between honest teachers seeking to look after the flock and others with alternative motives, such as popularity or self-justification. No amount of smiling, praising, or singing should hide a wolf in a church; we can know them by their fruits. Do they teach us to keep Jesus' commandments, or just wear the t-shirt?

We are taught to be fruitful Christians through the episode of the barren fig tree. A leafy Christian, who appears to be all singing and all dancing, will wither away on the Day of Judgment if they are found fruitless.

'*And when he saw a fig tree in the way, he came to it, and found nothing thereon, but leaves only, and said unto it, Let no fruit grow on thee henceforward for ever. And presently, the fig tree withered away.*' [Matthew 21:19; Luke 3:7–9]

Perhaps few messages from the Gospels are repeated more than this. The penalty for being a fruitless Christian is to be 'cast into the fire', but please don't panic! It is not a call for us to immediately be perfect in good works. Instead, we should be on the pathway to fruitful outcomes, and if we are slow walkers, then at least we are pressing forward with faith. The trees in my back garden do not yield fruit all year round. There is a time and a season for everything [Ecclesiastes 3:1–2], so our business is about growing fruit, not just harvesting. The key is to ensure we don't allow wolves or pesky squirrels to take the fruit of the gospel from ourselves or our children.

We must teach our children to plant the word in their hearts and help their seedlings grow in a good, wholesome soil environment. Simply teaching that the seed is good is insufficient in today's world of competing ideologies and social distractions. Using the following parable, Jesus taught the pitfalls that can stop the development of the gospel in the hearts of new-born Christians and thereby make them fruitless.

'*Behold, there went out a sower to sow: And it came to pass, as he sowed, some fell by the way side, and the fowls of the air came and devoured it up. And some fell on stony ground, where it had not much earth; and immediately it sprang up, because it had no depth of earth: But when the sun was up, it was scorched; and because it had no root, it withered away. And some fell among thorns, and the thorns grew up, and choked it, and it yielded no fruit. And other fell on good ground, and did yield fruit that sprang up and increased; and brought forth, some thirty, and some sixty, and some an hundred. And he said unto them, He that hath ears to hear, let him hear.*' [Mark 4:3–9]

The seed in this parable was always good, no matter where it fell, but the ground of our hearts has to be cultivated to provide a suitable environment for growth. The parable was given to help us see that the soil in our hearts should become more arable. The seed grows by God's grace, but we are expected to faithfully clear the field, always giving thanks to God for his gift of growth [Ephesians 2:8-10].

'I have planted, Apollos watered; but God gave the increase. So then neither is he that planteth any thing, neither he that watereth; but God that giveth the increase. Now he that planteth and he that watereth are one: and ***every man shall receive his own reward according to his own labour.****'* [1 Corinthians 3:6-8]

Fostering a home environment where we can be *'in the world but not of the world'* (a common extrapolation of John 17:15–16) will help provide our families with a lifeboat of safety from the storms of sin. A child can grow stronger if nourished by active—not passive—parenting. Remove the rocks, pluck out the thorns, and shine the gospel light upon your children. The counsel of Cinderella's mother holds true for parents who strive to raise their children in the gospel, 'Have courage and be kind.' [contained in Isaiah 41:6]

Like a plant, a child cannot be forced to grow strong; they can only be nourished, pruned, and protected by the kindness of your grace. Keeping the gospel's values consistently in the home takes parental courage.

Quick aside: *The name given to the first man on earth is Adam, which means 'Red Soil'. C.S. Lewis refers to mankind as 'Sons of Adam' [see Deuteronomy 32:8]. Hence, when Jesus talks about the different kinds of soil, he refers to the different types of children of men whose hearts can be cultivated through faithful discipleship. This was the case with John and Big James in 'The Chosen' episode one of season two.*

The following warning from the Sermon on the Mount is directly to the wolves.

'Not every one that saith unto me, Lord, Lord, shall enter into the kingdom of heaven; but he that doeth the will of my Father which is in heaven. Many will say to me in that day, Lord, Lord, have we not prophesied in thy name? and in thy name have cast out devils? and in thy name done many wonderful works? And then will I profess unto them, I never knew you: depart from me, ye that work iniquity.' [Matthew 7:21–23; Titus 1:16]

This scripture reminds me of the *Ghost of Christmas Present* from Charles Dickens' novel 'A Christmas Carol'. At 1 o'clock in the morning Scrooge is visited by his third instructor in an adjoining room. The Ghost tells him admonishingly,

'There are some upon this earth of yours who lay claim to know us, and who do their deeds of passion, pride, ill-will, hatred, envy, bigotry, and selfishness in our name; who are as strange to us and all our kith and kin, as if they had never lived.'

It is odd to think of religious teachers who espouse the gospel with their lips but whose hearts are far from him. Yet, we know this has been the case in so many windows that history opens to us.

'... well did Esaias prophesy of you, saying, This people draweth nigh unto me with their mouth, and honoureth me with their lips; but their heart is far from me. But in vain they do worship me, teaching for doctrines the commandments of men.' [Matthew 15:7-9]

The third commandment in Exodus is that we shall not take the name of the Lord in vain, but many take his name in vain when they confess him with their lips but reject his way of life. How sad it must be for our Heavenly Father to look down upon his children and see the rebellion of some of those who confess his name.

The fruits of the spirit spoken of in Galatians 5 are love [charity], joy, peace, longsuffering, gentleness, goodness, faith, meekness, and temperance. If we speak in tongues but lose our temper; if we cast out devils but care not for the widow; if we heal the sick yet neglect our children, then we are like a mirage springing up in the desert or an empty well.

'*These are wells without water, clouds that are carried with a tempest; to whom the mist of darkness is reserved for ever. For when they speak great swelling words of vanity, they allure through the lusts of the flesh, through much wantonness, those that were clean escaped from them who live in error. While they promise them liberty, they themselves are the servants of corruption*' [2 Peter 2:17-19].

The Apostle Paul gave a great explanation of what a Christlike life is and is not. If I had to save just a few passages of scripture to teach my children the way of the Lord, then 1 Corinthians 13:1-13 would be one of them.

'*Though I speak with the tongues of men and of angels, and have not charity, I am become as sounding brass, or a tinkling cymbal ...*'

When the High Priest ministered in the temple, they wore white garments underneath their robes. On the hem of the robe were *bells* of *pure gold* and *pomegranates* woven all the way around in sequence, one after the other [Exodus 39:24-26]. Dr. J Vernon McGee suggests that the bells represent our witness of Christ through our actions, as even though you could not see the priest inside the temple, you could hear him move. The Pomegranates represent the fruits of the spirit mentioned above in Galatians 5:22, the first of which is love. Each bell was surrounded by a pomegranate, suggesting that each action should be surrounded by love. Without the fruit of the spirit, our golden bells of service become *as sounding brass* or a *tinkling cymbal* as the scripture continues to explain,

... And though I have the gift of prophecy, and understand all mysteries, and all knowledge; and though I have all faith, so that I could remove mountains, and have not charity [love], I am nothing. And though I bestow all my goods to feed the poor, and though I give my body to be burned, and have not charity, it profiteth me nothing.' [1 Corinthians 13:1–3]

Notice how true charity is more than giving charitable handouts to people experiencing poverty. It is defined by who we are rather than what we do. Charity is a translation of *Agapen* (26), which means '*love*' or, more specifically, the '*divine love of Christ*'. Paul continues with this clarification.

'Charity suffereth long, and is kind; charity envieth not; charity vaunteth not itself, is not puffed up, Doth not

behave itself unseemly, seeketh not her own, is not easily provoked, thinketh no evil; Rejoiceth not in iniquity, but rejoiceth in the truth; Beareth all things, believeth all things, hopeth all things, endureth all things. Charity never faileth: but whether there be prophecies, they shall fail; whether there be tongues, they shall cease; whether there be knowledge, it shall vanish away. And now abideth faith, hope, charity, these three; but the greatest of these is charity.' [1 Corinthians 13:4–13]

This divine love of Christ is a gift that we should pray for. Each of us has room to improve, and perhaps nobody's failings have so frequently been revisited than that of Scrooge's lack of charity, which we hear each year at Christmas. Scrooge's heart changed when he saw a gravestone with his name inscribed.

'Spirit!' he cried, tight clutching at its robe, 'hear me! I am not the man I was. I will not be the man I must have been but for this intercourse. Why show me this, if I am past all hope?'

'Good Spirit' he pursued, as down upon the ground he fell before it: 'Your nature intercedes for me, and pities me. Assure me that I yet may change these shadows you have shown me, by an altered life! I will honour Christmas in my heart, and try to keep it all the year ... Oh, tell me I may sponge away the writing on this stone!'

We don't need Scrooge's three ghosts to appear in our bed chamber to have our hearts changed into the image of Christ, but we do need to pray in our *closets* for this divine love of Christ to fill our hearts. It should be desired more than any other gift. Perhaps nowhere in scripture is there a more perfect parable of how to apply these teachings in our lives than that of the Good Samaritan. The story has several layers, teaching us the need to love our neighbour and the plan God has for us [Luke 10:29-37]. This map within the parable will be expounded upon later in the next book, but for now, here are the final words of the Saviour after he taught the parable: *'Then said Jesus unto him, Go, and do thou likewise.'*

So, too, these are the things we must teach our fellow climbers, lest we become wolves in sheep's clothing.

The Rock

Nestled at the end of the Sermon on the Mount sits a gem of instruction that will never get old. Almost every child attending church has sung the song or heard the parable of the wise man who built his house upon a rock.

'Therefore whosoever heareth these sayings of mine, and doeth them, I will liken him unto a wise man, which built his house upon a rock: And the rain descended, and the floods came, and the winds blew, and beat upon that house; and it fell not: for it was founded upon a rock. And everyone that heareth these sayings of mine, and doeth them not, shall be likened unto a foolish man, which built his house upon the sand: And the rain descended, and the floods came, and the winds blew, and beat upon that house; and it fell: and great was the fall of it.' [Matthew 7:24–27]

Whenever I heard this parable sung in church, it reminded me that we should build our lives based upon Christ rather than the shifting sands of man's doctrine; however, I missed the main reason for the parable because I had heard it so much, I had become '**parable blind**'. The critical line was at the beginning.

'Therefore whosoever heareth these sayings of mine, <u>and doeth them</u>, I will liken him unto a wise man ...' [v.24]

There would be little point in me sitting at the feet of the Saviour and basking in his glorious light if I did not get up and do what he taught me to do. For those who sit at his feet each Sunday and then neglect his work, he says,

'And every one that heareth these sayings of mine, and <u>doeth them not</u>, shall be likened unto a foolish man which built his house upon the sand, ...and great was the fall.' [v.26–27]

The parable of the foolish man teaches against those who attend church each week with inverted cups, in the same way that the parable of the Ten Virgins denounces the five foolish ones who did not trim their lamps [Matthew 25:1-13]. All ten virgins were active church members, but only five did his will. The wise men and women are not those who give the most money, sit in the highest seats, or pray the loudest. The wise are those who hear the word of the Lord and try to do it. They will humbly ask on Judgment Day,

'... Lord, when saw we thee an hungred, and fed thee? or thirsty, and gave thee drink? When saw we thee a stranger,

and took thee in? or naked, and clothed thee? Or when saw we thee sick, or in prison, and came unto thee? And the King shall answer and say unto them, Verily I say unto you, Inasmuch as ye have done it unto one of the least of these my brethren, ye have done it unto me.' [Matthew 25:37-40].

Each time we remember the Sermon on the Mount, whether it be the wise man building his house, avoiding the wolves, loving our neighbour, or setting our light upon a hill, may we remember that Jesus was coaching us on how to <u>be</u> rather than dictating every action that we should do. We are on earth to demonstrate to God that where Jesus has gone, we want to follow and become joint heirs with him.

'*The Spirit itself beareth witness with our spirit, that we are the children of God: And if children, then heirs; heirs of God, and joint-heirs with Christ; if so be that we suffer with him, that we may be also glorified together*' [Romans 8:16–17; John 10:34].

It seems fitting to end this Sermon on the Mount review with the words of the Saviour from the book of Revelation. These are the words given in the last chapter of the New Testament, and they summarise who Jesus is and how he can bless us.

'I am Alpha and Omega, the beginning and the end, the first and the last. Blessed are they that do his commandments, that they may have right to the tree of life,

and may enter in through the gates into the city.' [Revelation 22:13–14; 19:8]

May we grow fruit on our tree and stand as a lighthouse with him at the top of the rock.

(See also Jeremiah 17:10; Matthew 3:10; 1 Corinthians 3:8–13)

Chapter Nine

Sunset

'Soon it will be dark, where there can be no more progress ... I press onwards and upwards, trying to use every last drop of the sun's light before it sets over the ridge'

On the first day of creation, the Lord caused there to be light; then, he divided the light from the darkness. The light he called 'day' and the darkness he called 'night'. It is often quoted that as surely as night follows day, certain things will come to pass, which Shakespeare used in Hamlet. Every part of life's university is leading up to the day when the sun will set, and no more work can be done. Pens down, please. Stop the climb and stay where you are!

'I must work the works of him that sent me, while it is day: the night cometh, when no man can work.' [John 9:4]

On the Day of Judgment, all people must stand before God and speak with him face to face. We will be in a physical, resurrected body, just like Jesus, and be able to abide in his presence long enough to give an account of our lives.

'For it is written, As I live, saith the Lord, every knee shall bow to me, and every tongue shall confess to God. So then every one of us shall give account of himself to God.' [Romans 14:11–12]

After giving God an account of our lives, we will receive judgment. At this time, we will be addressed by God, and I can imagine the verdict being read out to the just men and women of the earth as follows:

'Well done, thou good and faithful servant: thou hast been faithful over a few things, I will make thee ruler over many things: enter thou into the joy of thy Lord.' [Matthew 25:21]

The knowledge of Judgment Day should not fill our souls with fear. Our Saviour's mercy can stop justice pulling us down to a state of misery and endless torment. This is the meaning of being *justified*, as spoken of in scripture [Titus 3:7], where justice is overcome because Jesus was crucified.

I sometimes imagine that the word *justified* amalgamates the words justice and crucified. Due to his suffering on the cross and in Gethsemane, Jesus can absorb justice and bestow mercy. Another way to look at justification is that Jesus restores us to our previous condition (*Just if I'd* never sinned). He does not place us on a higher point of the climbing wall than before we fell but restores us to where we were. He does not do the climb for us, any more than the five foolish virgins were able to borrow oil for their lamps [Matthew 25:7-12]. His grace will catch us when we fall (*being saved*) and strengthen us to climb (*sanctification*).

Through this power of justification, he can choose to redeem us from our sins [Romans 3:24] or restore our former sins to us and cast us into prison, depending on our choices. Consider the parable of the servant who was forgiven a large debt. It is one of the most extended parables Christ gave and perhaps the closest to speaking in plainness—rather than parallelism—that we have. Jesus truly wanted us to understand this principle:

'Therefore is the kingdom of heaven likened unto a certain king, which would take account of his servants, and one was brought unto him, which owed him ten thousand talents. But forasmuch as he had not to pay, his lord commanded him to be sold, and his wife, and children, and all that he had, and payment to be made. The servant therefore fell down, and worshipped him, saying, Lord, have patience with me, and I will pay thee all. Then the lord of that servant was moved with compassion, and loosed him, and forgave him the debt.

But the same servant went out, and found one of his fellowservants, which owed him an hundred pence: and he laid hands on him, and took him by the throat, saying, Pay me that thou owest. And his fellowservant fell down at his feet, and besought him, saying, Have patience with me, and I will pay thee all. And he would not: but went and cast him into prison, till he should pay the debt. So when his fellowservants saw what was done, they were very sorry, and came and told unto their lord all that was done.

Then his lord, after that he had called him, said unto him, O thou wicked servant, I forgave thee all that debt, because thou desiredst me: Shouldest not thou also have had compassion on thy fellowservant, even as I had pity on thee? And his lord was wroth, and delivered him to the tormentors, till he should pay all that was due unto him.

So likewise shall my heavenly Father do also unto you, if ye from your hearts forgive not everyone his brother their trespasses.' [Matthew 18:23–35]

Which principle is repeated by Jesus during his final week,

'And whenever you stand praying, forgive, if you have anything against anyone, so that your Father also who is in heaven may forgive you your trespasses.' [Mark 11:25 ESV]

This echoes from the 'Lord's Prayer' taught on the sermon on the mount,

'And forgive us our debts, as we forgive our debtors ... For if ye forgive men their trespasses, your heavenly Father will also forgive you: But if ye forgive not men their trespasses, neither will your Father forgive your trespasses.' [Matthew 6:12-15; Ephesians 4:32]

The doctrine is found at the beginning, middle, and end of Jesus' mortal ministry. Three times, he teaches the need to forgive others in order to retain forgiveness ourselves. This principle is the embodiment of *Grace for Grace* [John1:16].

No matter how much God loves us, he has indicated he will not save us <u>in</u> our sins, only <u>from</u> them.

Being forgiven when we were born-again does not mean God cannot bring those sins back upon our heads if we fail to submit evidence of a change in our character. Opportunities to submit evidence are plentiful, whether through action or inaction.

'For if after they have escaped the pollutions of the world through the knowledge of the Lord and Saviour Jesus Christ, they are again entangled therein, and overcome, the latter end is worse with them than the beginning. For it had been better for them not to have known the way of righteousness, than, after they have known it, to turn from the holy commandment delivered unto them. But it is happened unto them according to the true proverb, The dog is turned to his own vomit again; and the sow that was washed to her wallowing in the mire.' [2 Peter 2:20–22]

Being forgiven is not the same as being righteous

Both forgiveness and righteousness are essential but separate ingredients on Judgment Day. The grace of Jesus Christ enables the obstacle of our sin to be removed, but it cannot falsify a good record, as that would be fraud, and God cannot lie. All of the virtues given in 2 Peter 1 are necessary for a person to become Christlike, and our time on earth is an opportunity for us to practice them. We will review the virtues in Part II, but for now, the attributes required on judgment day are as follows:

Faith, Diligence, Humility, Virtue, Knowledge, Temperance, Patience, Godliness, Brotherly kindness and Charity.

Ample opportunities arise each day for us to be like the Free Soloist, to climb as he would climb, and then evaluate our day in prayer to see if we have emulated the pattern of his love and kindness.

As C. S. Lewis reminds us in his Screwtape Letters: 'A moderated religion is as good for [the devil] as no religion at all.' [see also Revelation 3:15-16] Hence, we are encouraged to ponder our salvation in all gravity, determining what we should do and who we are becoming,

'Wherefore, my beloved, as ye have always obeyed, not as in my presence only, but now much more in my absence, work out your own salvation with fear and trembling.' [Philippians 2:12].

As with any experiment, we must consider the fruit of our labours each week and determine if we are going in the right direction or if we should be changing course. Prayer is a great time to evaluate our set of personal results. Taking the Lord's emblems on the first day of the week [Acts 20:7] gives us time to recommit to living as he would have us live and make adjustments when necessary.

The two grand keys of *grace* and *truth* unlock the gate of heaven to let us in. Being **saved by grace** is one grand key, and **obeying truth** is the other [Matthew 25:19-28]. Both need to fit on the Day of Judgment as if Christ had not died for our sins we would be eternally locked out of his kingdom, no matter how good our works have been [Ephesians 2:8–10], but without oil in our lamps, the door will remain shut to us [Matthew 25:7-12].

'But this I say, he which soweth sparingly shall reap also sparingly; and he which soweth bountifully shall reap also bountifully.' [2 Corinthians 9:6–8]

You may have started late or still have a long way to go, but don't worry. If we are wearing his graceful harness, clipped to his rope, and climbing his truth, he can lock off the rope and pull us up to meet him, even if darkness descends before we reach the top of the climb [James 4:10; John 6:40,44,54]. Perfection will take longer than our allotted time on the wall, so God cares more about which direction we are heading than our position. We are not judged on whether we have reached the top before death. A university student does not become an expert upon graduation, but an employer will know the direction they are moving in. Our judgment is to see if there is evidence that we are striving to reach the top, one handgrip at a time, rather than mosh around a campfire at the bottom. [Hebrews 12:1-11].

Chapter Ten

I Have Been Saved

There are approximately 31,000 Bible verses, equating to about half the number of polyamide fibres that comprise the twelve strands in a standard dynamic climbing rope. The rope only works if all the threads work together. Like these fragile fibres, I have had friends tell me they trust their eternal salvation, and that of their children, to two or three verses in the Bible. While hundreds of scriptures speak of the saving grace of the harness, how mighty it is to save, and how it will catch us when we fall, there are few, maybe two or three verses alone, that suggest we do not need to clip onto the rope and climb. Some have anchored their spiritual lives upon these two or three thin fibres.

Now I have been climbing for many years, I can answer the question about my own salvation. When I started, I didn't understand why people would ask if I had been saved. It seemed a strange question for someone starting out, but now I know the answer is a resounding YES! I was saved yesterday when I fell, along with last week and last month. All these years I have been climbing, I have been saved many times by the rope of his righteousness while wearing the harness of his grace. The rope has shown me the way and provided for my salvation when I stumble. If I wear his harness and stay clipped to the rope,

I will continue to be saved tomorrow [1 Corinthians 1:18]. I don't know if I will give up on the climb, unclip, and miss out on returning to his heavenly home at the top of the rock. I hope not, but each day is a new test of discipleship.

Jesus Christ is the Master Climber who has taken the fall for us as the sacrificial Lamb. I did not include this in the Parable of the Clip, but of necessity, we cannot neglect it. When Jesus anchored his rope for us at the top of the rock, he allowed Judas and the voice of the people to metaphorically throw him off the cliff, as they were desirous to do in his home town of Nazareth when he identified himself as the Messiah.

'*And they rose up and drove him out of the town and brought him to the brow of the hill on which their town was built, so that they could throw him down the cliff. But passing through their midst, he went away.*' [Luke 4:29-30]

His time was not yet, but he metaphorically allowed it when it did come so he might experience what it was like to fall from the highest point.

He made the perfect assent and now calls on us to use his rope. I am thankful for the covenant of the clip he extended to me and for his graceful harness. There are 31,000 verses in the Bible. Clip on and climb!

Epilogue

Two Christians were walking opposite ways along a dirt path; they met and drew upside-down arcs on the ground, which crossed each other at one place in the sign of a fish. While they were both the correct way up according to their different perspectives, they discovered their vantage point was less important than the faith they both drew from it. Jesus was standing in the middle of their faith, as he declared that when two or three are gathered together in his name, there would he be also [Matthew 18:20]. He reaches down gracefully, and we reach upwards with our faithful alms [Matthew 6:1]. I have seen great works performed by all Christians, whether they believe they are needed or not. They are lifting and blessing their fellow man all over the world! God knows our souls and can discern our hearts. If we struggle with questions, we can ask for guidance through the channel of prayer, which has a better range than any cellular network or satellite phone. This line of communication is open to all who climb the rock. In the Gospel of Matthew, we read,

'*Ask, and it shall be given you; seek, and ye shall find; knock, and it shall be opened unto you*' [Matthew 7:7 + James 1:5].

There is a God in heaven who loves you immensely. He sent his Son to die for you, preparing the way for your resurrection and forgiveness. If we strive to follow the way of his rope, we will enter into his presence.

Thank you for wading across the shores of Capernaum with me and getting deeper into the doctrine of Christ. We will close Part I by pulling our fishing boat onto the shore and resting for a season. '*Alpha: Harnessing Grace*' has been written to answer whether our salvation is assured by a simple confession of Jesus with our lips alone. I hope it has become evident that while we cannot be saved without the grace of the Lord Jesus Christ, we also need to become more like him so that we may enter his kingdom and feel comfortable at his table [Hebrews 12:11–17].

In Part II, we will swim a little further out to join Peter, who had the faith to walk on water with the Saviour. Conversion is a process, not an event, so Part II will guide us through all the elements of truth needed for a soul to successfully convert to Christ rather than just believe in him. Long after Peter confessed with his lips and believed in his heart that Jesus was the Christ, he was told, '*When thou art converted, strengthen thy brethren*' [Luke 22:32].

Our conversion is different from our belief. There is a path of sanctification we must follow, which Part II calls '*the way of truth*'. I will join you there after the supplements to Part I.

Captain's Log: Supplemental

TRINITY

an example of 5th century gaslighting and mansplaining

Have you ever seen people pondering over a piece of artwork hung on a wall or heard them commenting on poetry in a textbook? I am sure the original artists or poets would stand in amazement over the interpretations we come up with. We can sound intellectual and argue over several meanings when the truth could be far more simplistic.

THE ATHANASIAN CREED

(shortened version) circa 400–500 AD

We worship one God in Trinity, and Trinity in Unity; neither confounding the Persons, nor dividing the Essence. For there is one Person of the Father; another of the Son; and another of the Holy Ghost. But the Godhead of the Father, of the Son, and of the Holy Ghost, is all one; the Glory equal, the Majesty coeternal. Such as the Father is; such is the Son; and such is the Holy Ghost. The Father uncreated; the Son uncreated; and the Holy Ghost uncreated. The Father unlimited; the Son unlimited; and the Holy Ghost unlimited. The Father eternal; the Son eternal; and the Holy Ghost eternal. And yet they are not three eternals; but one eternal. As also there are not three uncreated; nor three infinites, but one uncreated; and one infinite. So likewise the Father is Almighty; the Son Almighty; and the Holy Ghost Almighty. And yet they are not three Almighties; but one Almighty. So the Father is God; the Son is God; and the Holy Ghost is God. And yet they are not three Gods; but one God. So likewise the Father is Lord; the Son Lord; and the Holy Ghost Lord. And yet not three Lords; but one Lord. For like as we are compelled by the Christian verity; to acknowledge every Person by himself to be God and Lord; So are we forbidden by the catholic religion; to say, There are three Gods, or three Lords... So that in all things, as aforesaid; the Unity in Trinity, and the Trinity in Unity, is to be worshipped. He therefore that will be saved, let him thus think of the Trinity... This is the catholic faith; which except a man believe truly and firmly, he cannot be saved.

If you are conjuring up in your mind's eye a picture of the Emperor in his new clothes walking naked down the street with all the crowds looking on, admiring how beautiful his clothes looked, then you would imagine the same reaction of people when they first heard this washing machine of words. Everything about the creed was generated by weavers of invisible fabric who tried to pass it off as exquisitely divine, sowing doubt and confusion. If you need a lawyer or a scientist to explain a principle of heaven, then the principle is not true. Some would like to declare that the Trinity is a holy mystery and say the oneness of God is unfathomable. Jesus spoke against this by saying:

'... It is given unto you to know the mysteries of the kingdom of heaven, but to them it is not given ... For this people's heart is waxed gross, and their ears are dull of hearing, and their eyes they have closed; lest at any time they should see with their eyes, and hear with their ears, and should understand with their heart, and should be converted, and I should heal them.' [Matthew 13:11–15]

Only One Lord & Saviour

Man created the trinity creed to explain the Bible's statement that there is only one God, but Jesus, being the Son of God, thought it not wrong to make himself equal with Him.

'*Therefore the Jews sought the more to kill him, because he not only had broken the sabbath, but said also that God was his Father, making himself equal with God.*' [John 5:18; Philippians 2:6]

Scripture states,

'*Hear, O Israel: The Lord our God is one Lord*' [Deuteronomy 6:4; Mark 12:29-32]

'*And ye shall know that I am in the midst of Israel, and that I am the Lord your God, and none else*' [Joel 2:27]

Jesus was aware of the doctrine but was not concerned with a contradiction as he was the God of the Old Testament. He was the King of Israel, the Lord their God, and their Saviour. He was the one who said, '*Hear, O Israel: The Lord our God is one Lord*'. He also had a Father whom he loved and looked to in everything he did.

In similitude, we each have one biological father on the earth, even though there are many fathers.

Jesus took upon himself the role of saviour and redeemer, as typified by the near sacrifice of Isaac. Thus, while Jesus was subject to the rule of his Father, he became the only saviour, the only redeemer, the only name under heaven whereby man can be saved, as stated in Isaiah 43,

'... *I am he: before me there was no God formed, neither shall there be after me I, even I, am the Lord; and beside me there is no saviour*' [Isaiah 43:10-15]

There is only one saviour, Jehovah, the Lord God of the Old Testament, who died for us. We have no other Saviour.

Peter emphasised the point,

'*Neither is there salvation in any other: for there is none other name under heaven given among men, whereby we must be saved.*' [Acts 4:12]

Jesus originally said,

'*I am the way, the truth, and the life: no man cometh unto the Father, but by me.*' [John 14:6]

Jesus has a Father whom we will all stand before on the day of judgment, but his Father (the Most High), has given Jehovah (Jesus), the kingdom of Israel.

'*When the Most High gave to the nations their inheritance, when he divided mankind, he fixed the borders of the peoples according to the number of the sons of God. But the LORD's portion is his people, Jacob his allotted heritage..*' [Deuteronomy 32:8-9 ESV]

Note: LORD is translated from Yahweh (3068) whom we call Jehovah, or Jesus.

God *the Most High* Father, gave his son, Jehovah, the kingdom of Israel (Jacob). They have no other god and no other king [John 10:31-36; Hebrews 1:1-2].

(for more detail on these scriptures, see the next book, *Distant Venom*)

Following his Father

Jesus taught that he did his Fathers will, not his own,

'*Father, if thou be willing, remove this cup from me: nevertheless not my will, but thine, be done.*' [Luke 22:42] *'I do nothing of myself; but as my Father hath taught me ... for I do always those things that please him.'* [John 8:28–29] '*So Jesus said to them, "Truly, truly, I say to you, the Son can do nothing of his own accord, but only what he sees the Father doing. For whatever the Father does, that the Son does likewise.*' [John 5:19 ESV]

He followed diligently in his Father's footsteps. Early Christian theologians have distorted the simple truths about God the Father and his Son to become a source of confusion between those who cry 'oneness' and others who call 'trinity'. As a collective body of Christians, we need to say, 'Stop! This is ridiculous.' As Jesus said before, '*Both shall fall into the ditch.*' [Matthew 15:14] We must return to Christ's original words and stop adding to his doctrine with our private interpretations.

Jesus acknowledged to his apostles that he was the Son of God and that his Father, who was currently in heaven, was his witness [Matthew 16:14–17]. We are informed that, after his death, he was to sit on the right-hand of his Father, the Most High.

'Who being the brightness of his glory, and the express image of his person, and upholding all things by the word of his power, when he had by himself purged our sins, sat down on the right hand of the Majesty on high.' [Hebrews 1:3]

It is interesting how many times we are told that Jesus would sit on the right-hand side of his Father in the heavens, not on his lap or inside his body, but on his right-hand side. Jesus taught that he lived with his Father in eternity before coming to the earth and wanted to return to be on his right-hand side when he had completed his mortal mission on earth, which he did [Mark 12:36; 16:19; Acts 2:32-33; Ephesians 1:20; Hebrews 10:12].

There are learned men from the early centuries of the church, after the death of the apostles, who '*desire to walk in long robes, and love greetings in the markets, and the highest seats in the synagogues, and the chief rooms at feasts*' [Luke 20:41–47]. Such men would have us recite creeds of dubious origin to explain a mystery that was never a mystery to a child [Luke 18:17]. Indeed, we cannot fathom the complexity of how a human child is created, let alone the vast universe. Still, we understand relationships as a child knows its mother, father, brothers and sisters. Hence, we can comprehend that Jesus is the literal Son of God.

The terms given in the Trinity creed matter not; what matters are the terms used by Jesus. Nowadays, people compare ice, water, and steam or use four-dimensional physics to explain the Trinity. They '*strain at a gnat, and swallow a camel*' [Matthew 23:24]. Jesus was very much aware of his Father's nature and called upon him in the family context. '*Abba Father.*' [Mark 14:36]

Be One

As Christians, we strive to be a united people of '*One Lord, one faith, one baptism, One God and Father of all, who is above all, and through all, and in you all*' [Ephesians 4:5–6]. I have often heard people discussing the Trinity by quoting this scripture in part but missing out on the last point: that, as well as there being one Lord, there is also one God who is the Father of us all. We are counselled to be *one* with both the Father and the Son and *one* with each other. The ship's captain should be at one with his crew, the architect with the builder, the choir with the chorister, and so on. Paul's epistle to the Philippians encouraged us to '*stand fast in one spirit, with one mind*' [Philippians 1:27]. He may have taken the inspiration for this call to be as '*one*' from the plea of the Saviour as he prayed before entering the Garden of Gethsemane:

'That they all may be one; as thou, Father, art in me, and I in thee, that they also may be one in us: that the world may believe that thou hast sent me. And the glory which

thou gavest me I have given them; that they may be one, even as we are one.'[John 17:21–22]

The concept that God, Jesus, and ourselves are all '*one*' is understood as being of one mind, heart, purpose, and doctrine.

Philip asked Jesus to show the disciples the Father, to which he replied:

'Have I been so long time with you, and yet hast thou not known me, Philip? he that hath seen me hath seen the Father; and how sayest thou then, Shew us the Father? Believest thou not that I am in the Father, and the Father in me? the words that I speak unto you I speak not of myself: but the Father that dwelleth in me, he doeth the works.' [John 14:7–13]

The word *seen* comes from *heoraken*, which means *to see with our mind's eye* or *see spiritually*, whereas the term *in* is translated from *en*, which denotes *power and blessing*, given figuratively from within. Paul used the same word to say how Jesus is 'in' him, and by extension, Jesus can be 'in' us as church members.

'*I am crucified with Christ: nevertheless I live; yet not I, but Christ liveth in me*' [Galatians 2:20]

The same principle is applied when writing to the Colossians. '*For in him dwelleth all the fulness of the Godhead bodily*' [Colossians 2:9].

It is eminently apparent we are not the same person as Jesus, but that Jesus figuratively lives in us in the same way the Father figuratively lives in him.

One Body

When Jesus said that married couples should be 'one flesh', he never intended us to have the same body or be the same person [Matthew 19:5-6]. Paul, however, expounded on this principle of unity when he addressed the saints in Corinth. He counselled the members to consider themselves as though they were all one body in Christ, in the same way, God and Jesus act as one.

'*But now are they many members, yet but one body ... And whether one member suffer, all the members suffer with it; or one member be honoured, all the members rejoice with it. Now ye are the body of Christ, and members in particular*' [1 Corinthians 12:20+26-27]

No church member has ever absorbed their body into the whole congregation. It has always been understood to mean we work in unity, as Jesus and his Father do. Paul uses this idea in his letter to the Romans, when he counsels them to be '*likeminded one toward another*' [Romans 15:4-5], which other Bibles translate as being of *one mind*, *complete harmony*, the *same point of view* or *in full sympathy with* each other. This harmony describes Jesus' relationship with his Father and all those who dwell in Zion.

The true nature of the Godhead was taught by Paul when he addressed the Corinthians,

'*But to us there is but **one God**, the Father, of whom are all things, and we in him; and **one Lord** Jesus Christ, by whom are all things, and we by him. Howbeit there is not in every man that knowledge*' [1 Corinthians 8:6–7].

This scripture could not be more precise in teaching that there is one God (the Father) and one Lord (Jesus Christ), and we are in them. Each time we take the sacramental bread and cup, we accept the invitation to dwell in Jesus and for Jesus to dwell in us [John 6:56]. While not all scripture is figurative, and much of it should be taken literally, specific ideas are manifestly metaphorical.

We can understand the perpetuation of the Trinity creed in times gone by, as scriptures were written in Latin and locked on the pulpits of the church, but now that we all have access to the word of God, we can look at the supposed mysteries of the past in a new light. Being 'one' means to be 'united' [Philippians 2:2].

***Note**: The bible has had some fake text added to it to help strengthen the case for the **oneness** of the Trinity, but scholars now agree that the fake scripture known as the 'Johannine Comma' should be removed. It is still found in the KJV version of 1 John 5:7-8, but thankfully, the ESV has removed it. The Johannine Comma shows the great lengths people go to weave the Trinity into scripture with their invisible yarn.*

Before and during the creation

We know that mid-flow during the creation, there is a pause while the Gods talk to each other and say, '*Let us make man in our image, after our likeness.*' [Genesis 1:26] The plural use of the terms '*us*' and '*our*' gives context to the book of Hebrews that, while one of the Gods may have been providing the command, they were both unified in one purpose during the creation.

'*God ... Hath in these last days spoken unto us by his Son, whom he hath appointed heir of all things, by whom also he made the worlds ... Your throne, O God [Jesus], is for ever and ever, the sceptre of uprightness is the sceptre of your kingdom. You have loved righteousness and hated wickedness; therefore God, your God [The Father], has anointed you [Jesus, the Son] with the oil of gladness beyond your companions.*' [Hebrews 1:1–3, 8–9 ESV]

Here, the most High God anointed his Son, Jesus, to be a God and heir of the kingdom. It was to this exalted station that Jesus was referring when he prayed after the Last Supper,

'*And now, O Father, glorify thou me with thine own self with the glory which I had with thee before the world was ... Father, I will that they also, whom thou hast given me, be with me where I am; that they may behold my glory, which thou hast given me: for thou lovedst me before the foundation of the world.*' [John 17:5+24]

Rather than being a prayer to himself or humanity metaphorically praying to a deity, this was a heartfelt heavenly phone call back home to his Dad, as the Son was about to pass through his final, painful set of tribulations. Jesus wanted to go back home when his work on earth was finished. They call upon us to become joint heirs and enter into their glory, which is why we were created in their image.

'*The Spirit itself beareth witness with our spirit, that we are the children of God: And if children, then heirs; heirs of God, and joint-heirs with Christ; if so be that we suffer with him, that we may be also glorified together.*' [Romans 8:16–17]

I did not come from myself

Jesus seemed to address the future trinity creeds when he declared that he did not come from himself.

'*... If God were your Father, ye would love me: for I proceeded forth and came from God; neither came I of myself, but he sent me. Why do ye not understand my speech? even because ye cannot hear my word*' [John 8:42–43]. (See also Matthew 3:16–17 and John 5:30–31)

The great test of Abraham in offering up Isaac [Genesis 22:10-12], the only begotten of Sarah, would have had little relevance in scripture if we were not to take from it the powerful symbol of a father offering up his son. So it is with the actual Father of eternity, offering up his only begotten Son, to become the Saviour of mankind. It was deeply personal.

Conclusion

Jesus taught that he was with the Father in the beginning, was his Son, and is now seated on his right-hand side. He taught that we can '*be one*' in the same way that he and the Father are 'one'. We are encouraged to understand, as a child does, the simple truths of the gospel rather than turning to the creeds of religious lawyers in the early centuries of Christianity. While the instigators of the creed claim to be built upon the rock of Peter, they are verily fabricated on the sand. When the flood of truth comes up from the earth, and the Reign of Christ comes down from heaven, we may find their houses washed away.

Stephen—the first Martyr after Christ—declared that the leaders of the people were ignoring the Holy Spirit, that their fathers killed the prophets, murdered the Son of God, and did not keep the law as it was intended. He was rushed upon and bitten by the leaders, who had become as rabid dogs. While being abused, he had a vision of the true nature of the Godhead.

'But he [Stephen], being full of the Holy Ghost, looked up steadfastly into heaven, and saw the glory of God, and Jesus standing on the right hand of God, and said, Behold, I see the heavens opened, and the Son of man standing on the right hand of God.'

Stephen was martyred after bearing his final testimony of the separate members of the Godhead.

'Then they cried out with <u>a loud voice</u>, and ***stopped their ears****, and ran upon him <u>with one accord</u>, and cast him out of the city, and stoned him.'* [Acts 7:54–58]

Though there were many people in this wicked council, they spoke with '*a*' single '*loud voice*' as though they were one person. They acted '*with one accord*' when they, as a group, stoned him to death. The devil told them to ***stop their ears*** from hearing the witness of Stephen, while they themselves acted as one body.

May we not stop our ears today

CROWN PRINCE OF JERICHO

There was a king who ruled in a beautiful kingdom, living in a palace filled with glory. He loved his citizens, and they honoured him as a graceful, wise ruler. The king wanted his subjects to grow and become more like him because he loved them. His son was obedient and did everything his father asked, growing up in the image of his father as he followed him.

The king told his son,

'*One day, you will inherit the kingdom, and I desire my subjects to help you rule and reign in righteousness, just as I have done [Romans 8:17]. They will need to learn, grow and be tested in all things so that you may know who to choose to rule with you [John 17:22; 1 Corinthians 6:2-3; Matthew 20:16]. Will you create a place where they might be taught truth and have the opportunity to practice living in the light of my way?*'

The son agreed to create a place to oversee the people, helping them grow and become great rulers, following their king's example. [Hebrews 1:2].

The king's voice then grew serious.

'*Son, my subjects will become dirty while they are away and cannot return to my kingdom in that state, for no unclean thing can dwell here, and they will suffer many afflictions. Their future king must pass through all their sorrows so that he may know how to help his subjects and atone for all their mistakes and follies so that they may be washed clean. This suffering will cause exquisite pain and deep distress.'*

The son freely offered to suffer for the people his father had given him, for he knew of the king's love for them. Under the king's direction, the son created a city called Jericho, to test the character of his subjects. In his unwavering obedience, the son went down to Jericho and did all his father asked, setting a powerful example for his subjects. He taught them the things his father commanded and revealed that if they were faithful, they would have the opportunity to rule with him. [Luke 19:16-19; Matthew 25:20-21; Mark 10:40-44].

Just before the son was to suffer the great tribulation of his people, he stopped and communicated with his father, the King, saying,

'*Father, I have glorified your name in the world and done all you asked me to do; please, therefore, grant that I may return to live with you, with the same glory I shared with you before I made the world, restored to your right-hand side.'* In the same communication, he also said, *'I ask that those whom you have given me may become one, as we father, are one, that we may all be one.'* [John 17; John 14:20]

--o--

Jesus did go and do all his Father asked of him and suffered great distress. The last thing he said to his disciples before they left their final meal together was,

'... *but I do as the Father has commanded me, so that the world may know that I love the Father.*' [John 14:15+21+23+27+31 ESV]

The Son showed the world that he was humble and diligent. He asks that we do the same in smaller, simpler ways. All who rule with the Son, whether over kingdoms or households, must do so upon the principles of righteousness, by persuasion, long-suffering, gentleness, meekness, unfeigned love, kindness and pure knowledge, without hypocrisy and without guile. They must be princes of peace.

'*And thou shalt teach them ordinances and laws, and shalt shew them the way wherein they must walk, and the work that they must do. Moreover thou shalt provide out of all the people able men, such as fear God, men of truth, hating covetousness; and place such over them, to be rulers of thousands, and rulers of hundreds, rulers of fifties, and rulers of tens: And let them judge the people at all seasons: and it shall be, that every great matter they shall bring unto thee, but every small matter they shall judge: so shall it be easier for thyself, and they shall bear the burden with thee.*' [Exodus 18:20-22; Matthew 25:21]

'*And he that overcometh, and keepeth my works unto the end, to him will I give power over the nations: And he shall rule them with a rod of iron [word of God] ... and I will give him the morning star. He that hath an ear, let him hear what the Spirit saith unto the churches*.' [Revelation 2:26-29; 2 Peter 1:19]

Note: The New Testament speaks of principalities, powers, thrones and dominions which refer to governments presiding over areas. It can imply a heavenly or earthly jurisdiction, or both. Principalities draws on the word 'principle', meaning first or chief. When we hear the word Prince, we often mean an heir to the throne, but sometimes the translation to Prince (*sar* 8269) in the Old Testament refers to a chief, ruler or captain. A Crown Prince is literally the next in line to become King. When God wrestled with Jacob in Genesis 32, his name was changed to Israel, which has two meanings: '*let God prevail*' and '*have power as a Prince*'. Indeed, God told Jacob the reason for changing his name,

'*Thy name shall be called no more Jacob, but Israel: for as a prince hast thou power with God and with men, and hast prevailed.*' [Genesis 32:28]

I think of the symbolism of a prince who humbly lets his Father's will prevail, or his Father's will be done, thereby increasing in favour with God and man. When we allow the will of the Father to prevail in our lives, we, too, become Israel or a Prince of heaven. Abraham's wife's name, Sarah, who is Israel's grandmother, means 'Princess'. Through this birthright, we are destined to become kings and queens, to rule and reign under the crown Prince's direction forever.

'Blessed are You, LORD our God, King of the universe'.

In heaven, there are many thrones: one for the Father, one for the Son, twenty-four thrones for ruling elders, and perhaps others we know not of [Revelation 4:4]. Each throne represents an area, the *Most High* being over all thrones in heaven and on earth, with lesser thrones subjected to the higher.

'*For by him were all things created, that are in heaven, and that are in earth, visible and invisible, whether they be thrones, or dominions, or principalities, or powers: all things were created by him, and for him ... that in all things he might have the preeminence.*' [Colossians 1:16-19; Hebrews 1:1-2]

Jesus is, therefore, the obedient Crown Prince, and we, his subjects, are being tested in Jericho to see if we will be obedient to him under all trials and circumstances. Those who increase their Christlike talents will be made kings and priests over principalities and powers in the world to come [Revelation 1:6].

'*His lord said unto him, Well done, good and faithful servant; thou hast been faithful over a few things, I will make thee ruler over many things: enter thou into the joy of thy lord.*' [Matthew 25:23]

PART II

Omega: The Way of Truth

With thanks to David Faulkner

‘It was Christ’s character

with His unique combination

of celestial attributes which

brought Him to and got Him

through Gethsemane and Calvary’

– Neal A. Maxwell

Content

Prologue

In Part I, we started climbing a rock face that the master climber—Jesus Christ—had scaled before us. He threw down a cyan rope, marking the path and providing safety should we fall.

There are three ways we could use the rope.

1) We could tie a knot on our harness and call for the person at the top to lift us up—no effort required, no increase of our talents. Just sit back and enjoy the ride.

2) We could tie two Prusik loops; put our feet in and slide upwards as we ascend the rope—no skill, no learning, just trust in the rope and go upwards.

3) We could climb the wall, following the path of the master climber as a disciple, learning his hand grips and developing spiritual muscles we never knew we had, becoming the image of the Free Soloist who ascended perfectly before us.

Of these three options, we will look at the third as we are disciples who follow him. In Jesus' day, many believed on his name because he gave out free stuff,

'*Jesus answered them and said, Verily, verily, I say unto you, Ye seek me, not because ye saw the miracles, but because ye did eat of the loaves, and were filled.*' [John 6:26]

During the last week of his ministry, some free-loaders rejected Jesus and called for his crucifixion, even though they confessed his name with their lips just days earlier. The path of faithful discipleship is not easy, yet when we trust in the Lord and join him with our whole souls, we can endure the trials of life. In the last known words we have of Paul before his death, he taught Timothy,

'*For the time will come when they will not endure sound doctrine; but after their own lusts shall they heap to themselves teachers, having itching ears; And they shall turn away their ears from the truth, and shall be turned unto fables. But watch thou in all things, endure afflictions, do the work*'. [2 Timothy 4:3-4]

Discipleship is not easy, but the grace of Jesus Christ is sufficient to strengthen us to bear all our afflictions. When Jesus suffered in the garden for our sins, an angel appeared to support him as he atoned for us. In the same way, the Lord will stand by to give us strength when we need him most, as written so perfectly in the Christian 'Footprints' poem.

The rope shows us the way up, not the way out.

A Plateau is the Highest form of Flattery

Having a plateau to rest on is a welcome relief during any long climb. One handgrip after another can become monotonous and draining. What starts as an exciting new challenge slowly morphs into mundane and routine. God knows this challenge and has put a plateau on the first day we climb every week. However, while we may take some sacramental bread and wine to revive ourselves, it is not a day for putting aside all work. The attributes of Christ require real spiritual effort to attain, and Jesus was constantly accused of doing this kind of work on the Sabbath.

'*... the Jews were persecuting Jesus, because he was doing these things on the Sabbath. But Jesus answered them, 'My Father is working until now, and I am working.*" [John 5:16-17 ESV]

While we rest from unnecessary labour, strenuous exercise, etc., on the Sabbath, our spiritual muscles are available 24/7. Throughout Part II, we will focus on the attributes that should never sleep, even when you are having a bad day. I often wonder if God allows us to have bad days so we can grow Christ's attributes in the same way people use resistance training.

The Way

την οδόν [LXX]

Jesus' disciples were not initially called *Christians* but called *the way*, which sounds weird in English, but that was the appellation we gave ourselves. Perhaps it is because, at the Last Supper, Jesus said,

'I am the way, the truth, and the life' [John 14:6]

After Adam and Eve partook of the fruit of the Tree of Knowledge of good and evil, they were cast out from the Garden of Eden. God commanded Cherubim (an angel of the temple) and a flaming sword (justice) to be placed at the east of the garden to guard '*the way*' to the Tree of Life [Genesis 3:24].

When Jesus performed his atonement in the Garden of Gethsemane and on the cross, he opened '*the way*' back to the Tree, enabling us to partake and live forever in his presence. We are told that at some point during the thousand years, perhaps at the end, a New Jerusalem will descend to the earth. Inside the edifice, before the throne of God, will be the Tree of Life [Revelation 21 + 22]. At the entrances to the city through the twelve gates made out of pearl, we may still find the angels standing there, guarding the way.

To pass by the sentinels, we will need to qualify, as described by John,

'*Blessed are they that do his commandments, that they may have right to the tree of life, and may enter in through the gates into the city.*' [Revelation 22:14; 19:8]

Jesus showed us *the way* to the Tree of Life through his teachings and opened up the *gates* through his suffering and death.

The Narrow Way

There is an interesting choice of words in Matthew where Jesus says,

'... *strait is the gate, and narrow is the way, which leadeth unto life, and few there be that find it*' [Matthew 7:14].

The term *strait* is *stenos*, which means narrow, but the word for *narrow* is *thlibo*, which means 'narrow through compression'. So, we could read the verse as,

'*narrow is the gate, and even narrower is the way.*'

After the wealthy young man asked a question—and did not like the answer—Jesus said,

'*And again I say unto you, it is easier for a camel to go through the eye of a needle, than for a rich man to enter into the kingdom of God.*' [Matthew 19:24]

The way is narrow, and one often feels compressed when following the master. It is hard, but there is no other way under heaven whereby we can be saved. I distinctly remember being asked on the day of my baptism if I felt excited, to which my answer was 'no', as I knew the commitment I was making. I was taking the name of Christ upon me, and entering into a covenant to strive to follow him. I did not want to take the name of Jesus upon me in vain, so it had to be a sober decision. That was a hard choice but also an easy one, as is often the case with Christianity, where we find dichotomies in harmony. This was the way, and there was no other way.

Isaiah prophesied that John the Baptist's mission was to include the declaration, '*Prepare ye the way of the Lord, make his paths straight*' [Matthew 3:3]. We, now, are to preach the narrow way taught by Jesus and make his paths straight as we prepare for his second coming and become a people fit to meet him. In this instance, *straight* is spelt the usual way, which indicates the need to correct crooked teachings and live uprightly sooner rather than later. The Greek word used grows from *euthus* (2117), which has an air of urgency.

John's teaching helped convert a devout Jew named Apollos, who taught the gospel as best he understood it with great vigour, yet when the missionary couple Aquila and Priscilla heard him, they felt the need to take him aside and correct *the way* he was teaching a little.

'*they took him unto them, and expounded unto him the way of God more perfectly*' [Acts 18:26].

By more perfectly explaining *the way* to him, they were helping to straighten the paths of the Lord.

Christians

The term *Christian* was first used at Antioch,

'*And when he [Barnabas] had found him [Paul], he brought him unto Antioch. And it came to pass, that a whole year they assembled themselves with the church, and taught much people. And the disciples were called Christians first in Antioch.*' [Acts 11:26]

The name *Christian* may initially have been a derogatory term coined by the people of Antioch to describe the crowds who were becoming converted to *the way* of the Lord. Antioch was the first main assembly area for Christians outside Jerusalem and was the starting point of Paul's missionary journeys. You can imagine the residents getting frustrated with the influx of people, so they gave us a name.

A Christian believes in Jesus and follows his teachings.

'*If any man serve me, let him follow me; and where I am, there shall also my servant be*' [John 12:26]

'*And he said to them all, If any man will come after me, let him deny himself, and take up his cross daily, and follow me.*' [Luke 9:23]

As Jesus is the way, the truth, and the life [John 14:6], we sometimes hear people who follow him described as people who walk in truth. We are saved from our sins when we are justified, and when we walk in his truth we are sanctified.

'For I rejoiced greatly, when the brethren came and testified of the truth that is in thee, even as thou walkest in the truth. I have no greater joy than to hear that my children walk in truth.' [3 John 1:3-4; 2 John 1:1-4]

'This is the way' – Din Djarin. The way of Truth.

Repetition on the Wall

The way marked by the rope has many handholds to lift ourselves and toe grips to support our stance. As touched upon earlier, these holds have names:

Faith, virtue, knowledge, temperance, patience, brotherly kindness, godliness and charity, with a special mention of humility and diligence.

It is important to remember that these grips repeat themselves many times along the way. Some are far apart, and others close; they can be in the same order or different, but however they appear, they repeat themselves as we climb. We start off looking at faith, but when we get to the end attribute of charity, we will need to start back at the beginning and reach for the next layer; just as an igloo rises from the snow to wrap around itself, layer upon layer until all blend into the final keystone at the top. Each climb stage is marked by a Sabbath plateau where we can rest and reflect on where we have been and where the rope goes next. You could ask yourself each week if your harness of grace is still clipped to the rope, and if you need to thank the Lord for catching you when you recently fell.

Those who embody the ten attributes given above will have become perfect, finished, or sanctified after washing their garments in the blood of the lamb. *The way* marked by the rope moves heavenward. To become perfect is to become finished, which is why we begin.

New-born to Adulthood

A new-born Christian is like a young child who strives to grow up to become a 'man' or 'woman' in Christ as they wisely apply the scriptures,

'*And that <u>from a child</u> thou hast known the holy scriptures, which are able to make thee wise unto salvation through faith which is in Christ Jesus ... That the <u>man of God</u> may be perfect, throughly furnished unto all good works.*' [2 Timothy 3:15-17]

We move from spiritual childhood to adulthood as men and women of Christ through applying the scriptures to our daily actions. Without this repetition, we remain spiritual infants in God's sight [1 Corinthians 13:10-11]. The world will define a man or woman in many ways, but we have a measuring stick to define the stature of a perfect man or woman as follows,

'*Till we all come in the unity of the faith, and of the knowledge of the Son of God, unto a perfect man, unto the measure of the stature of the fulness of Christ*' [Ephesians 4:13]

Attaining knowledge of the Son of God is more than knowing about him, for even the devils know about him and believe [Matthew 8:28-31; James 2:19]. Assimilating the attributes we are to discuss in Part II moves us from knowing about Jesus to knowing him personally through becoming like him. He grew into perfection over time, *'And Jesus increased in wisdom and stature, and in favour with God and man.'* [Luke 2:52], but never once did he sin along the way [Hebrews 4:15]. We are also expected to grow into perfection but need the redemptive power of the Lamb's blood to wash us from our sins (falls) as we climb.

Another descriptor that represents the Greek word for perfection is 'mature', which illustrates our journey from being a new-born Christian to spiritual adulthood. This journey is akin to a child following their father or mother, a process that scripture describes with the word *mimétés*, which is the root of 'mimic' or 'mime artist'.

'*Be ye therefore followers (mimickers) of God, as dear children*' [Ephesians 5:1]

Just as children mimic their fathers to become like them, we too are called to mimic the Saviour. This is how we grow into perfection, by actively following his example and teachings.

Quick aside*: Jesus commanded, 'Be ye therefore perfect, even as your Father which is in heaven is perfect'. The Greek word for 'perfect' is teleios (5046), which means 'complete', 'fully grown', and 'mature'. The Latin word 'integritas' is where we get the term 'integer', meaning a whole number, but it is also the root of the word 'integrity'. In English, integrity means to be perfectly honest and upright in character, and in Latin, it means to be 'one'. I like wordplay, so if I were to create a motto for my household, it would be 'teleios integritas', meaning* *'perfect integrity' or 'completely whole', which is the miracle that Jesus can perform in our lives when we become 'one' with him. Perhaps I should symbolically write* ***teleios integritas*** *across my heart.*

The Way of Purchasing Olive Oil

Before we knuckle down on how to climb the wall, I want to introduce you to—or remind you of—the parable of the ten virgins. Jesus established this frame of reference, which we should always keep in the back of our minds.

'*Then shall the kingdom of heaven be likened unto ten virgins, which took their lamps, and went forth to meet the bridegroom. And five of them were wise, and five were foolish. They that were foolish took their lamps, and took no oil with them: But the wise took oil in their vessels with their lamps. While the bridegroom tarried, they all slumbered and slept.*

And at midnight there was a cry made, Behold, the bridegroom cometh; go ye out to meet him. Then all those virgins arose, and trimmed their lamps. And the foolish said unto the wise, Give us of your oil; for our lamps are gone out. But the wise answered, saying, Not so; lest there be not enough for us and you: but go ye rather to them that sell, and buy for yourselves.

And while they went to buy, the bridegroom came; and they that were ready went in with him to the marriage: and the door was shut. Afterward came also the other virgins, saying, Lord, Lord, open to us. But he answered and said, Verily I say unto you, I know you not.' [Matthew 25:1-12]

The ten virgins were there to bring the church (the bride) to Christ's house for the wedding. One purpose of the bread and wine is to remind us that Jesus had gone home to his Father to prepare a place for us in His mansions, as promised at the Last Supper.

'*In my Father's house are many mansions: if it were not so, I would have told you. I go to prepare a place for you. And if I go and prepare a place for you, I will come again, and receive you unto myself; that where I am, there ye may be also.*' [John 14:2-3]

This was Jewish custom that those engaged to be married drank wine together in public and then the groom would go away for a time to prepare a place for the marital home. Only when the Father said the house was ready would Jesus (the groom) be allowed to marry, and come out to meet the bride (covenant Israel), with messengers sent before him to call the bride and her entourage to the marriage. We are betrothed or engaged to Christ when we partake of the emblems of his body, but none of us have been to the wedding yet, as we are to carry the church heavenward at the last day. This is when the wedding will occur, and we must be ready for that great and terrible day. Great for those with oil in their lamps but terrible for those who have failed to purchase it in time.

All ten virgins were church members and had confessed wholeheartedly with their lips that they believed the Lord was coming, even though he seemed to delay his arrival. It was in the middle of the night when the call came, and they excitedly went to meet the groom, but five of the watchful church members were not ready. They were lacking oil in their lamps. Those who were called to be the light of the world were good for an hour or two at church, but any longer than that, their lights would go out. They asked to borrow from fellow church members who could not lend their oil, as we cannot share Christlike attributes gained from serving others. The olive oil had to be purchased at a price not by the bridegroom but with their own money.

Cross-reference Jesus' teaching about the need to be a wise virgin (follower) and his sermon about the wise man who built his house upon the rock. Andrea Woodmansee taught me that the parable of the wise man was preceded by the same judgement we find at the end of the parable of the wise virgins. Take the time to compare Matthew 7:23-24 with Matthew 25:10-12 and ask why Jesus included two parables about wise followers.

For those who were invited, but not ready, the Lord said '*Verily I say unto you, I know you not*', and the door was shut to them. Furthermore, we are told that some who make it into the house will not wear the wedding garment as commanded, so they will be thrown out. [Matthew 22:11-14 + Revelation 19:7-8].

'*Omega: The Way of Truth*' is written to help us develop (or purchase) oil for our lamps and describes how to put on the wedding garment.

The Ten Attributes

(climbing grips)

THE FIRST TWO

HUMILITY

DILIGENCE

THE NEXT EIGHT

FAITH

VIRTUE

KNOWLEDGE

TEMPERANCE

PATIENCE

BROTHERLY KINDNESS

GODLINESS

CHARITY

[2 Peter Chapter 1]

HUMILITY

(John 3:30)

One might fret that the task of assimilating the attributes of Christ is a huge rock face to climb, and they would be right. When one understands the magnitude of the task ahead, it is expected to feel overwhelmed and daunted; yet this is the beginning of 'humility', and no person can gain all of the attributes of Christ without first acquiring it. In the Beatitudes, we are counselled to be poor in spirit, which means humility.

Humility is our willingness to submit to the will of the Son, just as the Son was willing to submit to the will of the Father and give him the honour. The grace of the anointed is sufficient to make weak things become strong to the humble who follow him. One cannot become perfect, complete, or whole [*teleios integritas*] without the enabling power of the atonement of Jesus Christ. When we recognise our dependence on him, we can humbly reach out and sincerely ask for help.

The Humble Transistor

Transistors use a small amount of electricity to open a gate and allow a large amount of current into the system, like opening the sluice gate on a dam, which opens a breach, allowing the powerful water behind to flow through. Opening the windows of heaven to have blessings poured out upon us requires humility and is often demonstrated through giving offerings.

'*Bring ye all the tithes into the storehouse, that there may be meat in mine house, and prove me now herewith, saith the Lord of hosts, if I will not open you the windows of heaven, and pour you out a blessing, that there shall not be room enough to receive it.*' [Malachi 3:10].

The widow who cast her two mites into the temple treasury is the best example of this type of offering (if you don't know the story, please read Luke 21:1-4). While nobody around her knew the sacrifice she made, the Lord knew, and now the world honours her unwritten name.

'... *before honour is humility.*' [Proverbs 15:33] The antithesis of which is pride, thinking we are Christlike enough already. [Matthew 23:11-14; Luke 18:11-14 + 20:46-57]

2 Peter chapter 1 focuses on nine attributes, but in the previous epistle, Peter closes with an instruction on humility. He asks us to be clothed with humility and gives the following reason: '*for God resisteth the proud, and giveth grace to the humble*' [1 Peter 5:5]. Therefore, the first qualification for God's enabling grace is humility.

Peter continues, '*Humble yourselves therefore under the mighty hand of God, that he may exalt you in due time*'. The attributes spoken of in the chapters ahead are all about getting ready for exaltation in the due time of the Lord, where our election becomes assured.

Jesus demonstrated humility in many ways [John 5:30], but most notably in Matthew 26:38-39 when he submitted to the excruciating will of the Father to pay for our sins.

James teaches that we must show humility to receive grace,

'*But he giveth more grace. Wherefore he saith, God resisteth the proud, but giveth grace unto the humble*' [James 4:6].

Regarding humility, Jesus taught,

'*When thou art bidden of any man to a wedding, sit not down in the highest room; lest a more honourable man than thou be bidden of him; And he that bade thee and him come and say to thee, Give this man place; and thou begin with shame to take the lowest room. But when thou art bidden, go and sit down in the lowest room; that when he that bade thee cometh, he may say unto thee, Friend, go up higher: then shalt thou have worship in the presence of them that sit at meat with thee. For whosoever exalteth himself shall be abased; and he that humbleth himself shall be exalted.*' [Luke 14:7-11]

As we seek to attain Christ's attributes, we first acknowledge that we need his help, thereby sitting down in the lowest room. Let us not beguile ourselves by saying we have enough faith or enough patience already. Once we have achieved a primary level of an attribute, we can then use that to acquire a secondary level, then press forward to achieve a college level, a university level, and so on until we are perfect in that attribute. Expert levels are gained through years of 'on-the-job' experience, which a school or university graduate can only glimpse at. Imagine a young student mocking an old cabinet maker, 'All you need is a saw, a few screws and a bit of sandpaper' might be the taunting accusation. The expert craftsman would not even bother replying.

DILIGENCE

(Luke 11:9)

Pressing forward with a steadfastness in Christ is the principle of 'diligence', which is essential in developing all the other attributes we will discuss. Peter stated, '*And beside this, giving all diligence, add to your faith virtue; and to virtue knowledge ... etc.*'. Without diligence, nobody would find what they are looking for [Luke 15:8]. Once found, diligence is the glue that holds all the attributes in place. Diligence means constantly striving to achieve a goal and is the opposite of a 'once saved, always saved' culture. Diligence begins with separating oneself from the mattress in the morning and permeates each action until the going down of the sun. Of course, we take breaks, and of course, we cannot exclude those in latitudes that only have a few minutes of sunlight during the day, but hopefully, you catch the feeling. Diligence is the lifeblood of accomplishment in any endeavour and is fuelled by hope.

The Webster's Dictionary of 1828 is a gold mine for understanding the old language used in the KJV. Diligence has several definitions, but here it means 'constant effort to accomplish what is undertaken'. This is the way we should approach all the attributes, with unwavering, determined effort each day, accepting that we will fail and falter along the way.

While diligence covers a myriad of endeavours, I want to focus on one for a moment, which is the king: Prayer.

Every attribute of Jesus Christ can be achieved in small or large quantities, which is why even seemingly wicked individuals can possess a few good qualities [Matthew 5:46]. Sometimes, characteristics of Christ can be faked, in a similar way a passport can be faked, but under trials, we find flaws in our own (or others) half-baked characters. God shows us our weaknesses so we can focus on these areas to make them strong. **This is done in the first instance, through prayer**. When we seek to improve an attribute, we start by praying with all the energy of our hearts for help, which is an act of spiritual creation. Prayer is the king endeavour, as most spiritual achievements begin with prayer or a considered articulation to God. If we are specific with him, he can be straightforward with us. Wishy-washy prayers get wishy-washy answers. Earnest prayers, filled with genuine emotion and commitment, yield meaningful and powerful results.

'*And I say unto you, Ask, and it shall be given you; seek, and ye shall find; knock, and it shall be opened unto you. For every one that asketh receiveth; and he that seeketh findeth; and to him that knocketh it shall be opened.*' [Luke 11:9-10] '*The effectual fervent prayer of a righteous man availeth much.*' [James 5:16]

Prayer is where we seek to align our will with God's will, not vice versa.

Add

Peter said '*And beside this, giving all diligence, add to your faith virtue ... etc.*'

The word 'add' is translated as 'supplement' elsewhere, reminding me of my wife, who takes vitamin supplements daily. A vitamin is something our body needs but cannot generally create itself, so it must be gained from external sources. Similarly, we require spiritual supplements to become more like our Saviour, and these don't come by accident but rather by choice. A wholly 'natural man' would not have any attributes of Christ in their character, but a holy 'spiritual man' would have them all. If we desire to supplement our lives with Christlike attributes, we must choose that way of life rather than accidentally acquiring them. One does not evolve into a Christian by natural selection.

Every person born into this world has the light of Christ given to them in some degree, whereby they can feel the difference between right and wrong, such that, when they are of age, they can discern truth from error. However, if a person ignores these pulls towards righteous living long enough, they grow further from the light of Christ towards spiritual darkness. Often, it takes an awakening for someone to '*come to themselves*' as was the case with the prodigal son, who made a concerted effort to change and improve after hitting rock bottom (see Luke 15:17-18).

We must consciously take our spiritual supplements daily to avoid becoming oblivious to spiritual matters and waste our time in riotous living. Remember that spiritual supplements do not naturally occur in our bodies, just as essential vitamins do not. While reasonable people exhibit several godly characteristics, very few have them all. Nevertheless, with all the energy of our hearts, we must pray each day to be nourished with these supplements and come to a fullness of the knowledge of Christ's character.

The ten spiritual supplements we strive to assimilate are easier to remember if we use the first letter of each attribute to help repeat them in our minds, like a Bible Bee ... FVKTP BkGC (HD). When we acquire and manifest each of these, we will have become purified, even as Jesus is pure. This is the way.

'*Beloved, now are we the sons of God, and it doth not yet appear what we shall be: but we know that, when he shall appear, we shall be like him; for we shall see him as he is. And every man that hath this hope in him purifieth himself, even as he is pure.*' [1 John 3:2-3; 1 Peter 1:22].

Part II aims to define these vital supplements and suggest ways to acquire them.

We must diligently pray to add the attributes of Christ to our daily lives. We mimic and try to become more like him as we serve him. You may feel like a fraudster and have imposter syndrome, but God rewards a hypocrite who tries to be like Jesus more than a hypocrite who thinks they already are [Luke 18:9-14].

Consider *Humility* and *Diligence* as being a prerequisite for each step you take towards the next eight attributes.

FAITH

(James 2:22)

It seems strange to ascribe the attribute of faith to Christ, as he was divine from the beginning. However, in this section, we are not addressing whether Jesus believed or knew there was a God; we are looking at his faithfulness to God, just as God is faithful to us. Therefore, we will focus on faith as a verb rather than a noun.

Faith is 'Belief in Action'

The Latin root for belief is *creditis*, from which we get the idea of a good credit score. It means that when we *believe* someone, we *trust* what they say.

A famous use of *belief* is in John 3:16,

'*For God so loved the world, that he gave his only begotten Son, that whosoever believeth in him should not perish, but have everlasting life.*'

The Greek word used here is *pisteuo* (4100), which, like the Latin, means to *trust* someone. When we believe in Jesus, we trust that we should do all he told us to do because he has a 100% *creditis* score!

When *belief* is used in the Old Testament, such as when Moses saw God in the burning bush and was worried others might not believe him, the Hebrew word *aman* (539) is used, which means to *confirm* or *support*. It is close to the word *amen* (543) we use today after a great sermon or prayer, to which we all say 'amen' or 'so be it'. The word in Hebrew between these two (541), is also *aman*, meaning *turn to the right*. Moses wanted the people to support his words and *turn to the right*, but sadly, they did not always do that. When we believe in Jesus, we *turn to him* and *follow him*.

The words for *belief* and *repent* have a significant element of *turning* in them.

Another use of the word *belief* in scripture is Romans 10:9-10 which supports the idea of trusting and turning to righteousness.

'... *if thou shalt confess with thy mouth the Lord Jesus, and shalt believe in thine heart that God hath raised him from the dead, thou shalt be saved. For with the heart man believeth unto righteousness; and with the mouth confession is made unto salvation.*'

Other translations for this verse state,

'*for in the heart is belief <u>unto</u> righteousness*' (Berean Literal Bible)

'*for with the heart a person believes, <u>resulting</u> in righteousness*' (NASB) '*for with the heart a person believes, leading to righteousness*' (Legacy Standard Bible)

These translations show that belief, correctly followed, leads to change, in the same way that a compass, correctly followed, leads to a destination.

When Jesus told us to be baptised, we trust him enough to be baptised. When he said to repent, we repent; to forgive, we forgive; to clothe the naked, we clothe them, starting with our own families. Belief becomes Faith when quantum entangled with action.

If Jesus told you there was a bomb in your house and that you need to follow him to safety, you would probably believe him, as you give a high credit score to his words. Without following him, believing he was right would not save you from the bomb. This is how belief leads to salvation: trusting him enough to follow him.

Peter said,

'*... Neither is there salvation in any other: for there is none other name under heaven given among men, whereby we must be saved.*' [Acts 4:10-12]

There is no other name whom we can trust our salvation to.

The woman who had an issue of blood for twelve years was healed because she pressed forward towards Christ, exercising faith rather than sitting at home and believing the stories she heard. Jesus said to her,

'Daughter, thy faith hath made thee whole' [Mark 5:34]

While belief is the solid ground on which we stand, it can achieve nothing on its own, just as the ground beneath our feet is static and will not take us anywhere. Imagine a football placed in the middle of a soccer pitch. You may believe your team will put the ball in the back of the net, but unless they kick it, the stadium will have no joy, only disappointment. A baseball provides no fun if the pitcher holds the ball for three hours without throwing it. You may believe that God is real, but your belief will not take you any closer to living with him unless you put it into action. Joy comes when you throw the ball, and angels cheer you on as you run.

Quick aside: *The Greek word for 'servant' or 'minister' is diakonos (1249), which means 'to kick up dust as you run an errand'.*

Faithful

The translation of the word *faith* from Greek or Hebrew to English is the same as the word *faithful.* The Old Testament only mentions the word *faith* a few times in the KJV, but most other translations use *faithfulness* in its place. I have a friend called Eamon, who I consider my 'faithful friend' as his name reminds me of the Hebrew word *emun*, which means *faithful.* Even God refers to himself as '*the faithful God*', so this is certainly a principle of heaven, not just an attribute for our time on earth [Deuteronomy 7:9].

Faith is the active link that joins belief to knowledge. Nestled between these two bookends of a Christian journey is the attribute we live with daily. We start *believing* in Jesus, and after pressing forward in *faith*, we eventually come to *know* him. Once a person believes there is a God who sent his Son into the world to show us the way, that person has a decision to make ... do they act on their belief, or do they remain as they are?

Jesus said, '*he that is greatest among you shall be your servant.*' [Matthew 23:11] and a tiny mustard seed of faith '*is the greatest among herbs, and becometh a tree*' [Matthew 13:32]. We are supposed to grow our faith, and the key to growth is through the principle of faithful service.

We speak of 'an act of faith', 'a step of faith', or even taking 'a leap of faith' more than we talk of faith on its own [James 2:17-20]. When Harry Potter took his leap of faith through the station wall onto platform nine and three-quarters, Mrs Weasley encouraged him by saying, '*Best do it at a bit of a run if you're nervous*'. There's no substitute for throwing yourself in and following Christ. The only difference between an aeroplane taxiing slowly on the ground and one soaring through the heavens is the thrust (trust) it is producing. You don't get anywhere by standing still on the runway, no matter how much your passengers believe.

Faithfulness through gaining Talents

To move on from mere belief towards faithful action, we need to look at the parable of the talents.

'*For the kingdom of heaven is as a man travelling into a far country, who called his own servants, and delivered unto them his goods. And unto one he gave five talents, to another two, and to another one; to every man according to his several ability; and straightway took his journey. Then he that had received the five talents went and traded with the same, and made them other five talents.*'

So far so good. You get a blessing and you work on doubling it.

'*And likewise he that had received two, he also gained other two*'

Again, even though he started with less, he still doubled it.

'*But he that had received one went and digged in the earth, and hid his lord's money.*'

Oh, bother. You can read on with the parable, but I can promise it doesn't end well for the person who buried their talent. The person believed his master had given him something special, but he buried it in the ground. The ground represents our belief in God, as he correctly trusted it would be safe there, but keeping your talent buried is the opposite of faith. During the sermon on the mount, Jesus said, '*Let your light so shine before men, that they may see your good works, and glorify your Father which is in heaven.*' The talent represents the knowledge of God we receive through service, which service glorifies God [Ephesians 2:10].

As Peter said regarding the attributes of Christ,

'*if these things be in you, and abound, they make you that ye shall neither be barren nor unfruitful in the knowledge of our Lord Jesus Christ.*'

We seek to get to know our Lord, not just believe in him. The parable of the sower and the parable of the talents finish with Jesus saying the same thing,

'*For whosoever hath, to him shall be given, and he shall have more abundance: but whosoever hath not, from him shall be taken away even that he hath.*' [Matthew 13:3-12; Matthew 25:14-29]

This principle has two parables dedicated to it because it is essential for a Christian's growth. Belief in God doesn't do anything on its own; if left dormant, that which we have will be taken from us. Faithfulness generates improvement and maturity in Christ.

'*Moreover it is required in stewards, that a man be found faithful.*' [1 Corinthians 4:2]

Cold Mornings and Dark Nights

I have been a Christian for many years and had the opportunity to try to serve God in several different capacities. I have worked primarily with youth, served as a missionary, and counselled with several leadership teams. The discipleship pathway is sometimes fun but mostly harder than sitting on the sofa and watching TV. I don't go to church because I enjoy it; I don't go for the sociality, nor do I go because it is the only place I can learn the gospel. Serving the Lord by serving his children is not passive; hence, the term *faithfulness* involves action.

The natural man in me would like to turn up to church on a Sunday, take the emblems of his body & blood, then leave after a few good songs and a talk. However, this would make me a couch potato Christian who only wants to be fed, like one of the five thousand, rather than a standard bearer who raises the Ensign. Jesus does not keep sheep so they can get fat and fall over. He is the good shepherd; we are his sheep and have a purpose to fulfil. Persistent couch potatoes rarely have talent, and it is the talents we gain through service that Jesus said will fuel our final judgment [Matthew 25:29-30]. Some of the sheep the shepherds kept on that starry night when the Saviour was born were ultimately going to be offered to the Lord as a sacrifice in the Temple. We could ask the Lord what sacrifice we should be making. Are we leaving the '*ninety & nine*' to go after '*the one*' as the shepherd(s) did? [Matthew 18:12-13; Luke 2:15-16]

I say this because I don't want anybody to think the path of faithful discipleship is easy. It demands time, energy and talents, even if your abilities are small. Talents grow through service. You are probably already doing better than you think:

- Checking on your neighbour.
- Phoning a friend.
- Sitting next to a solitary person at church.
- Inviting a family over for dinner.
- Inviting someone to a church activity
- Going for a family walk
- Posting uplifting & unifying thoughts on social media
- Helping at a church group.
- Volunteering in the community
- Having patience with people you meet

You should not beat yourself up if you struggle to leave the couch, as just getting to church can be an ordeal for some people. See that all these things are done in wisdom and order, for it is not requisite that a man should run faster than he has strength. What matters is that we gently stretch ourselves and strive to become more like Jesus. A gymnast cannot do the splits in a day, and a tree does not grow in a year; it takes time, but remember that a piano key pressed too softly produces no music.

The service we give produces fruit <u>inside us</u> and multiplies our talents. Good works are the mechanism whereby we develop the intrinsic fruit of a Christlike nature. All external fruit is a by-product of that process. Our changed nature enables us to become more profitable to God. As we climb higher, the attributes become more embedded in our character through repetition.

Our works reflect our character, but, as suggested before, we cannot fake a good report just by doing good work. God can see deep inside our soul, so those like the hypocrites of old will not pull the wool over God's eyes just because they are dressed in sheep's clothing [Matthew 6:1-5; 7:21-23]. We serve to get to know our master rather than earn salvation.

'*And this is life eternal, that they might know thee the only true God, and Jesus Christ, whom thou hast sent.*' [John 17:3]

Even if we served him perfectly from now on, our service would never pay for our sins. We cannot be justified through service, but equally, we cannot be genuinely sanctified without the personal growth that comes from it.

Cold mornings are difficult; dark, rainy nights are intimidating. These tribulations enable us to gain spiritual muscles in places we never knew we had. Step by step, principle by principle, we can become better today than yesterday. One day for church and six days for fun makes one weak, so let us use the other six days to justify our rest on the Sabbath. Expect to make mistakes, expect to embarrass yourself, expect to wish you could crawl under the covers and not emerge until it is all over. These are normal, natural Christian feelings. I am sure Mary sometimes sat on Jesus' bed and listened to his cries about how hard it was to '*increase in wisdom and stature, and in favour with God and man'* [Luke 2:52].

Conclusion

Faith is better translated as faithfulness, a verb, a doing word. As noted at the beginning, some dictionaries will place *faith* in the context of *belief* as a noun, and I can understand this, but it only sometimes fits the biblical narrative. It is written,

'But without faith it is impossible to please him: for he that cometh to God must believe that he is, and that he is a rewarder of them that diligently seek him.' [Hebrews 11:6]

Therefore … *faith = belief + diligence*

It is the substance of things hoped for and the evidence of things not seen. By faith, the elders obtained a good report, the earth was formed, sacrifices were made, prophets were translated, a giant arc was built, an inheritance was given, heavenly cities were sought, and children were conceived & delivered. [Hebrews 11:1-12]. The gospel plan revolves around faith, which principle will help us get to know the character, perfections and attributes of God.

Note: *Some mistakenly feel their faith will lead to wealth. Hope in God's promises should not be hope for monetary rewards [1 Timothy 6:5-7]. A person who is being honoured by becoming a 'joint heir' with Christ would look for ways they can be a net contributor to the cause, although, admittedly, when we have served God in the least, we are blessed in some way and continue to be* *indebted to him. When paying offerings to any church, ensure your tithes and donations are auditable.*

We must not extend ourselves into dangerous situations when helping our fellow man. 'Health and Safety' should not be put aside in any regular act of service. In addition, we should be constantly aware of the need to safeguard ourselves and others from false accusations and temptations [2 Timothy 3:2-3]. I have thrice seen how the kind gestures of church members have led to family breakups and shattered hearts. The rule of never being alone with someone else's wife or husband should not be ignored, even in service. A teacher should never be alone in a class with children, nor give them unaccompanied lifts in cars or vans.

VIRTUE

(Proverbs 31:20)

When discussing virtue, we should remember that language, over time, can become diluted in some areas and concentrated in others. While we use the English vocabulary to communicate ideas, the root words from which our language evolved (etymology) have had a long journey to arrive in our dictionaries. Usually, we use the word 'virtue' to describe sexual purity, which is one aspect of it; however, there are deeper connotations which should be considered as a whole. While Part II focuses on the attributes of Christ as assigned by Peter, we could also call them the 'ten virtues', as virtue can mean a characteristic or attribute, demonstrated by the common phrase 'patience is a virtue'. In this section we will look at virtue as its own attribute.

'Virtue' derives from the Latin *vir,* meaning *man,* and *tutem* or *tutor,* meaning *protector* or *guardian*. Thus, the image of a virtuous man who keeps people safe in the face of battle has filtered into various military medals throughout the centuries. The Latin word *virtus* literally means *strength*, so it follows that a virtuous man would use his strength to protect, defend or guard a woman's chastity, honour and home. The Hebrew word *chayil* (2428), translated as 'virtue' in many of our Bibles, also has connotations of strength and protection.

Proverbs 31:10, for many people, has been a scripture to encourage sexual purity in their daughters, as it reads,

'*Who can find a virtuous woman, for her price is far above rubies*', yet the rest of the chapter deals with attributes of wealth, industry and hospitality rather than simply describing sexual purity alone. The same chapter goes on in verse 29 to bookend the description of virtue by reminding the reader what the whole chapter has been describing,

'*Many daughters have done virtuously, but thou excellest them all.*'

If we were to consider the writing style as a chiasm—a literary device that involves repeating words, phrases, or ideas in forward, then reverse order, with the main point in the middle—then the centre point of virtue would be somewhere between verses 10 and 29, which is verse 20,

'*She stretcheth out her hand to the poor; yea, she reacheth forth her hands to the needy.*'

While it is not a definitive chiasm, it is structured well enough to highlight how virtue involves protecting the weak and providing for their needs. The declaration that Ruth was a virtuous woman is preceded by the arduous task of gleaning the fields in Ruth 2, which causes Ruth 3:11 to be spoken by Boaz. So, being virtuous involves working hard on causes related to serving others.

(See supplement 'Ten Camels' at the end of Part II)

Healing Virtue

One famous use of virtue by Jesus is when he healed a woman,

'... *a woman having an issue of blood twelve years, which had spent all her living upon physicians, neither could be healed of any, came behind him, and touched the border of his garment: and immediately her issue of blood stanched ... And Jesus said, Somebody hath touched me: for I perceive that virtue is gone out of me.*' [Luke 8:43-46; Luke 6:19]

The word 'virtue' used here (1411) is translated differently in other versions, but all have the same connotation of an inherent power, which comes from somethings nature. It reflects strength, ability and the might of an army. The virtue that healed the woman was the power of God, so, just like Ruth, virtue involves protecting, healing, and blessing the lives of others to the degree we have the capacity to perform. As Peter said when he was able to heal the lame man by the temple, '*Silver and gold have I none; but such as I have give I thee*' [Acts 3:6].

When we lend strength to helping and protecting others, we exercise virtue.

Moral Standards

A 'Standard' is a flag around which people gather, whether in peace or at war. In his letter to Timothy, Paul stated, '*But if any provide not for his own, and specially for those of his own house, he hath denied the faith, and is worse than an infidel.*' [1 Timothy 5:8] It is the provision for those in our family or those over whom we have influence that defines our basic virtue. As our virtue increases, we desire to reach out and bless other people within our sphere of influence. Morality is our ability to know right from wrong in any setting, and virtue is our ability to act morally.

It is a matter of integrity when we act morally both at home and abroad. We can judge right from wrong in society if we first start by considering the effect of our actions on our family. Jesus' teachings help us move out from the comfort zone of our family alone and sublimate our standards into society at large, whether or not they choose to follow Christ. The people around us will hopefully be kinder to each other through their association with us. Usually, even wicked people will love their family members selflessly. Morality is projecting that same familial love onto others we influence in a social or congregational setting. On the whole, what is right and wrong in our family will, by extension, be naturally right or wrong in society. Therefore, moral standards could be defined as Family Standards for Society [Matthew 5:47].

Hopefully, I will die before my daughters do. Seeing the lovely old ladies in church, I often imagine how I would treat them if they were my daughters. I would be so sad to see my children as widows—alone and struggling—that, of course, I would want to invite them into my home to love and comfort them. One day, the old lady across the street at number 26 could be my own daughter. In the grand scheme of heaven, each old lady you see could easily have been born to you in the future rather than to some other person in the past. God will judge us in considerable measure on how well we treat the widows, the poor, and the needy in society.

'*Pure religion and undefiled before God and the Father is this, To visit the fatherless and widows in their affliction, and to keep himself unspotted from the world.*' [James 1:27]

They are all God's children, and in different times, under other circumstances, they could have been your children, too. Ruth was a young widow who cared for Naomi, an older widow, which epitomises the very attribute we are discussing here. This kind of morality, projected into society, is the basis of virtue as the second great commandment presses us, '*Thou shalt love thy neighbour as thyself*', so we could equally say, '*Thou shalt love thy neighbour as thine own kin*', but more about that later.

The greater your desire and ability to help your neighbour, the greater your strength of virtue.

Sexual Purity

If we consider virtue as an extension of the commandment which forbids adultery or sexual relationships outside of marriage, then we would be correct to associate such a law with this principle. A virtuous person brings honour and strength to a home, whereas improper sexual conduct brings dishonour. Remember, the Ten Commandments should be treated as eternal principles rather than specific laws from which a loophole searcher can find cracks. The

613 laws in the Torah were available to be twisted by Pharisees who wanted to get out of their obligation to parents, etc. [Mark 7:10-13]. Jesus addressed this issue when he gave the sermon on the Mount by taking the specific rule of not committing adultery and expanding it to the root of not lusting after women in general. The higher law was about enhancing the Ten Commandments.

If you have ever fallen victim to your lusts or gone further, as in the case of the woman taken in adultery, remember that Jesus counselled her to '*go, and sin no more*'. [John 8:11; Matthew 10:38]. The path is narrow with ditches on either side, but the word of God stands as an iron rod running the entire length of the course. If we stay close to the word we will find it harder to fall. One must have power over their natural urges, keeping them within the bounds the Lord has set, to be considered virtuous.

Just before the attributes of Christ are listed in 2 Peter 1, we are told that to be partakers of the divine nature, we must escape the corruption in the world brought about by lust, which lusts are the unbridled desires of the natural man. There is a difference between *divine* and *natural* nature. When our natural nature becomes subject to our spiritual nature, we will have overcome the world (*see section on 'Temperance'*). It is one of the battles a virtuous person must win. Marriage between a man and woman is ordained of God and is encouraged for the appropriate, kind and considerate use of the powers of creation.

While Part II is taken from the soil of 2 Peter Chapter 1, there is strong counsel given by Peter in Chapter 2 to counter those who '*walk after the flesh in the lust of uncleanness*'. Chapter one extols exalting behaviour, while chapter two rebukes debasing behaviour. They are set side by side for a reason.

Conclusion

I like the Latin root of virtue, which describes a person who defends and guards. I like the virtuous story of Ruth, who provided for her family in difficult times. I am comforted by the knowledge that Christ's virtue can heal me now and in the future. I know the virtue of the word of God is more powerful than a two-edged sword [Hebrews 4:12]. If there is anything virtuous, lovely, of good report or praiseworthy, we seek after these things [Philippians 4:8].

KNOWLEDGE

(John 17:3)

As Jesus grew through his teenage years and into adulthood, he increased in wisdom, which has its foundation in knowledge. When Jesus was tempted at the end of his forty days of fasting, he used scripture to defend against scripture. If Jesus did not know better, he may have been influenced to jump off the wall of the temple to prove to Satan his true position as the Messiah [Matthew 4:5-7]. Not only had Jesus treasured up knowledge of Gods will, but he had taken the time to ponder how to apply that knowledge wisely.

Hunger and Thirst after Knowledge

I don't know if the following story is true, but if it isn't, it should be.

A young man approached the Greek philosopher and stated, *'O great Socrates, I come to you for knowledge'.* The philosopher took the young man down to the sea, waded in with him, and dunked him under the water. When he let the young man up for air, Socrates asked him to repeat what he wanted. *'Knowledge, O great one,'* he spluttered. Socrates put him under the water again, only this time a little longer. After repeated dunking and responses, the philosopher asked, *'What do you want?'* The young man finally gasped, *'Air. I want air!'. 'Good,'* answered Socrates. *'Now, when you want knowledge as much as you want air, you shall have it.'*

Now, imagine that we do the same with everyone who desires baptism. We take them to the water and immerse them. '*Why did you want to be baptised?*' we ask as they come up. '*To join the church'*, they might say—wrong answer. The correct answer is '*I want to get to know Jesus Christ by following him*', and baptism is just the beginning of his commandments.

In the Beatitudes, we are counselled to hunger and thirst after righteousness, which is an excellent way to describe our attitude towards gaining knowledge. Hungering and thirsting for something conveys an earnest desire rather than a vague interest.

Knowledge of God is the tree we seek in the field of life, while still recognising the need for other good types of knowledge to become well-rounded individuals. Our earthly university requires this knowledge to graduate, which is not gained from simply reading books on the subject. The knowledge we gain through studying the life of the Saviour is but the embryo, or seed that needs to be nourished through real-world experiments rather than remaining in academia.

The Psalmist encouraged us to move from simply knowing a subject to understanding it when he said, *'The meditation of my heart shall be of understanding*' [Psalm 49:3]. So, the knowledge we receive will only sprout into understanding by pondering how to apply it.

There is a gap between knowledge and understanding; in the same way, wisdom differs from facts. **Knowledge**

approaches understanding, but understanding sheds knowledge. A child who is only taught answers will know that 2 + 2 = 4 but will only see the broader implications of mathematics by pondering the subject, practising lots of other examples, and gaining the light of understanding. Knowledge will remain in its infancy and understanding will stand far away, unless time and effort are put into a subject. As the Psalmist wrote: *'A good understanding have all they that do his commandments'* [Psalm 111:10].

A father does not teach a child to ride a bike by reading him a book, nor does a helicopter pilot learn to hover by watching the instructor at the controls. A new mechanic would have to be shown how to fix something, whereas an experienced mechanic would know how to fix a fault he has never seen because he understands the whole system. This is the type of knowledge we seek through faithful hands-on service (see James 1:22 & Hosea 14:9). 'Knowledge' spoken of in the New Testament is derived from the Greek word *gnósis* (1108), which means knowledge or wisdom gained through experience, rather than learning by rote (repetition). *Gnosis* is the route of the word *science,* where many practical experiments are used to solidify and expand knowledge [Proverbs 3:13].

When Paul wrote to the Colossians, he reviewed the relationship between serving the Lord and getting to know him when he said,

'For this cause we also ... desire that ye might be filled with the knowledge of his will in all wisdom and spiritual understanding; That ye might walk worthy of the Lord

unto all pleasing, being fruitful in every good work, and increasing in the knowledge of God' [Colossians 1:9-10].

Just as butter is made by churning the cream of milk over and over, when we take an aspect of Christ's character and churn it over in our minds, we develop a greater understanding of the principle. When we act on the principle again and again, it solidifies into our characters, just as the milk solidifies into butter [Hebrews 5:12-14].

We might read a book or hear a lesson which contains thousands of words, but the principles we take from those words can be distilled into a few short concepts. These mindful concepts cannot always be spoken but change our lives. As Proverbs 2:1 starts by encouraging us to '*hide my commandments with thee*' or '*treasure my commandments within you*', so we distil the knowledge gained from keeping the commandments until it becomes a treasure within us that is hidden (see Proverbs 2:1-11). Jesus was the best teacher for unfolding these treasures of knowledge through parables, yet we still need to incline our hearts to understand and unpack the gift of knowledge he has given us. A parable can be heard and repeated, yet not understood. Even the early disciples needed Jesus to expound some of the parables to them [Luke 8:8-11].

To quote T.S. Eliot once again, '*We shall not cease from exploration, and the end of all our exploring will be to arrive where we started, and know the place for the first time*'

So it is when we study, ponder, and receive the light of understanding from heaven, as the light of Christ illuminates truth. The more light we receive, the more we know, and the more we practice what we know, the more light we will receive, growing brighter and brighter until that perfect day [2 Peter 1:19].

I don't know if it helps, and I cannot say we are a perfect example, but here are some practical things we do in our family to help increase knowledge,

- We pray each morning and night, individually and as a family
- Each person is encouraged—but not forced—to read a chapter of scripture a day
- We listen to talks from trusted people
- We discuss those things we have learned at church and in personal study
- We send screenshots of scriptures which have impressed us to each other
- One night of the week, we guarantee to be together, have fun and learn
- We play scripture games, such as *'Who am I?'*
- We laugh at ourselves and enjoy learning
- We forget sometimes; life gets busy, and then we start again

Here are some things we do to apply knowledge

- We attend church and participate in the lessons
- We actively participate in extended family life

- We assist the family in looking after older members
- We have older people at church whom we watch over and help where needed
- We share the gospel whenever the opportunity arises
- We are active in the community
- We do our best at work
- We have wholesome hobbies
- We help out at church, including cleaning up after activities
- We fail, make mistakes and get disheartened.

Like on Instagram or Facebook, it might seem that we or others are doing great, but behind the scenes, we can be just as muddled up and stressed as everyone else. I guess the secret (if there is one) is to talk of Christ, rejoice in Christ, preach of Christ and write those things we have learned in journals so that our children (and grandchildren) will know where to look for a remission of their sins.

Scripture does not say eternal life is gained from knowing <u>about God</u>. Scripture, the church, and our families are vehicles that help us get to know <u>God personally</u> by taking up our crosses and following him.

We can be sanctified no faster than we gain knowledge of Christ,

'*And this is life eternal, that they might* ***know thee*** *the only true God, and Jesus Christ, whom thou hast sent.*' [John 17:3]

This knowledge is gained from studying, pondering, and applying Christ's attributes through service to family, friends, and others [2 Peter 3:18].

Jesus gave the parable of the sower in Mark 4:3-9 as one of his first-ever teaching episodes. His disciples asked him what his words meant, so he explained it to them in Mark 4:110-20. Think of the parable as it relates to gaining knowledge of Christ like a seed that grows in your heart's good soil. As you protect and nourish the word, it will grow into greater understanding. You will know the seed is good as it sprouts and produces fruit you can taste. As you continue to nourish, it will become a tree of life for you.

'*The fruit of the righteous is a tree of life*' [Proverbs 11:30]

This type of knowledge is the light of truth, or the light of Christ, and is the greatest of all knowledge. When others see our fruit, they see the light of Christ reflected in us. Light and Truth are the 'righteousness' we hunger and thirst after [Matthew 5:6]. This is the way. Lux Veritas x

(see *Parable of the Little Olive Tree* at the end of Part II)

TEMPERANCE

(1 Corinthians 9:25)

Scriptural temperance is not just about anger. It means submitting the natural urge to the spiritual. The KJV translation of *egkratei* (1466) into 'temperance' springs from the concept of self-mastery or self-control. In the Beatitudes, we are counselled to be meek, which is 'strength and power under control', so it is that we submit our natural will to our spiritual will.

Quick aside: *Humility is submitting our spirits to God, while Temperance is submitting our bodies to our spirits.*

The Temperance movement in 1920s America, which promoted abstinence or severely restricted alcohol consumption, is an example of how temperance has long been associated with controlling the natural man.

We could also 'temper' clay, which makes it easier to mould by adding water and allowing it to stand still for a while. Isaiah declared to God, '*we are the clay, and thou our potter; and we are the work of thy hand*' [Isaiah 64:8]. As clay, we are moulded into the people God asks us to become, not by force or power but by gentleness, persuasion and love. To become a suitable clay-like substance for the master to mould, it sometimes helps to stand still for a while and bathe in his living waters [Psalms 46:10], helping us hold back from natural impulses. Indeed, as in Galatians 5:23-24, temperance is one of the fruits of the Spirit, and those who have 'crucified the flesh with the affections and lusts' will have become temperate.

Those who seek to change others with power or anger work opposite to the fruit of the Spirit and oppose the plan of salvation offered to us in the Gospel of Jesus Christ. No power or influence ought to be maintained by any church or family leadership position except through persuasion, gentleness and kindness. There is no justification for any person in authority to lose their temperance while seeking to correct another.

Temper Opinions

Before we explore controlling anger or the misuse of power, let's look at how temperance affects our thoughts. It is easy to become extreme in one's opinion when we feel we are on the right track. Many terrorists have acted out of passion for their version of the truth, while some political proponents have used underhand tactics or lied to further their cause. When one has the truth or knows the person who is the way and the truth, they should act moderately.

Jesus was accused of not keeping the Sabbath, but it was his understanding of the Sabbath, mixed with temperance, that made him no harsh extremist. He was the most qualified to have a strict opinion, yet he sought to influence with love and understanding rather than a loud voice or railing accusations [2 Peter 2:10-13].

'*And he said unto them, The sabbath was made for man, and not man for the sabbath: Therefore the Son of man is Lord also of the sabbath.*' [Mark 2:27-28]

Here, Jesus showed that he was not a Pharisee whose observance was legalistic but used the teachings of the prophets correctly rather than mechanically. Temperance can stop us from becoming the kind of religious fanatics who crucify our Lord while thinking we serve him [John 16:2; Acts 7:52]. Temperance puts the commandment to love God and our fellow man above a rule, regulation, or quota.

Jesus said,

'*Woe unto you, scribes and Pharisees, hypocrites! for ye make clean the outside of the cup and of the platter, but within they are full of extortion and excess*' [Matthew 23:25]

Excess of religiousness was their Achilles Heel, which Satan bruised, but Jesus crushed.

Paul said, '*Let your moderation be known unto all men*' [Philippians 4:5].

As Christians, we can become overzealous and want to chop Malchus' ear off with our words of defence [John 18:10], but we should more often than not choose to show love and kindness.

Temperance and the Ten

Of the Ten Commandments, we have the first and foremost responsibility to love God and our fellow man, which may need us to adapt the other commandments. For example, we are to honour our parents (#5) and love our heavenly Father (#1), so if our parents tell us we are crazy for going to church as adults, even though we seem to be dishonouring them in the short term, we should choose to love God first. Later, as time passes, our parents and other family members will see the honour we bring them.

Jean Valjean famously stole a loaf of bread to feed his sister's child, who was close to death. He broke commandment #8 but honoured the second greatest commandment in the law by doing so.

In accepting that some commandments should be enforced while others relaxed at certain points [Mark 2:24-26], there is no excuse for breaking a commandment because we find it inconvenient or challenging. Jesus understood the spirit in which the law was given, and hence, he used temperance when deciding how to apply the law. This discernment is a gift of the Spirit which should be prayed for [1 Kings 3:5-12]. Indeed, wisdom and temperance are travelling companions. Only when we are voluntarily a keeper of the law of faith are we entitled, under inspiration, to make an exception.

Did Jesus ever get angry?

We find an interesting translation in the KJV version of the sermon on the Mount, recorded in Matthew 5:22.

Along with not killing anyone, Jesus said we should not be angry with our brother. However, the KJV translators may have thought this was too hard, so they added a bit. They said, '*whoever is angry with his brother* *without a cause* *shall be in danger of the judgment*', but all other translations do not include '*without a cause*'. Jesus meant what he said when he taught us not to be angry with our brother and gave us no excuse. We should be temperate by not losing our cool, or taking things to excess, including anger or any other extremes.

If we look at Jesus' cleansing of the Temple during his last week in Jerusalem, we see him casting out the money changers from his Father's house, overthrowing tables and chairs to make his point. People had entered against the principles of the law to carry out unholy practices within its walls. Yes, the moneychangers needed to be there so that temple currency could be used, and doves were also required to be sold to those who wanted to make offerings, but the compound of the Temple was not the place for these transactions. A mechanic does not set up a garage in his front room – unless you're my wife's granddad; nevertheless, he got in trouble, too.

At times, a temperate person would have to go to war, yet such a one would not slip into the depravity of war seen so much in history. Temperance is demonstrated through meekness, which (as mentioned before) is power under control. One might have an intruder in their home, but rolling a hand grenade into the front room to stop them from stealing a TV would not be a suitable response. Our earth life is a test, and holding back our natural urge to lash out is a big part of the trial. Going to war is sometimes necessary, but only ever a last resort. If we use a hand grenade to stop a thief, then we could lose our own house and family in the destruction that follows. As Malachi says in chapter four, the Lord will leave the wicked '*neither root nor branch*', which means our family will be removed from us, and we will be left alone in the world to come if we cannot control our thoughts, words or actions [Matthew 18:25].

Let the course of action you take be commensurate with the level needed to solve the issue. There are occasions where a person may give their adversary what they desire and double it, such as the teaching from the sermon on the Mount [Matthew 5:38-44]. Almost every martial arts master would teach their students to walk away from trouble rather than escalate a conflict. If an armed thief desires your wallet, let him take it rather than risk your life. Martial arts are there to defend, not attack. When someone threatens your family or country, you have the right to respond. If someone talks to you in a tone you disagree with, you can walk away.

If you look at your family circumstances, are there any long running family feuds where you may be in the right, but the measurement of your punishment has led to disproportionate results. The measure we use to dish out our displeasure to others when they are in the wrong will be the same measure of justice that God uses to recompense us for our wrongs against him; vengeance for vengeance and grace for grace [Luke 6:35-38].

Going back to Jesus and the money changers, he had the power to call down legions of angels to cast everyone out of the Temple and restore order, yet he chose to make a small whip of chords and turn over some tables and chairs. While some people had to stand up rather than sit down, we can be assured that no doves suffered from dizziness, for the tables they were placed on were not turned over [Matthew 21:12]. If you see a film that depicts Jesus losing his temper, it is not accurate. With the total power of the universe at his disposal, Jesus made a point while remaining calm and in control of his body.

Stopping a child from burning themselves on a hot iron may require us to teach a lesson quickly and firmly. Still, whether they burn their fingers or not, we must be able to immediately embrace them with love, having them feel protection and kindness rather than wrath.

Chill for a bit

Another example that sheds light on temperance is regarding the woman taken in adultery. Jesus came to the Temple early in the morning and was teaching when the Scribes and Pharisees brought before him a woman who was taken in the act of committing adultery. It always baffles me why they did not get the man as well, as the law required both to be put to death [Leviticus 20:10], but I guess they wanted to blame the woman and protect themselves, as they, too, were adulterers in Jesus' eyes [Matthew 12:38-39]. Anyway, here was the woman presented before Jesus, and the leaders of the people wanted to trap him and accuse him of violating the law. So far, Jesus had healed the sick and raised the dead, but would he now condone the death sentence? All eyes were on him, and the people were ready, in their wrath, to stone the woman. Pause for a moment and imagine the ill feeling, hot temper, and readiness of the people to strike. The law stated that you needed two witnesses, and only those witnesses could cast the first stone [Deuteronomy 17:6-7], but equally, the witnesses could choose to walk away.

Nobody knows what Jesus wrote in the dirt that day, but he stooped down and started to write with his finger. The people probably thought he was preparing an answer and waited for his reply. Interestingly, the finger which wrote the Ten Commandments on stone, including the commandment against adultery, was now writing in the dirt. Rather than writing something to educate the people, he acted like he hadn't heard the question. Maybe he used the time to reflect on how his step-father Joseph would have felt when it was discovered Mary was pregnant. Persistently, they asked him again.

After he had distracted them long enough and time had passed, he lifted himself and spoke the immortal words, '*He that is without sin among you, let him first cast a stone at her*'. He then stooped down and continued writing. If I am wondering what he was writing, the people were also distracted enough to wonder, thereby defusing themselves from their anger. What did Jesus say? He who has no sin, let him cast the first stone.

The people started to disband, starting from the eldest, who would have known they were guilty of many sins and perhaps were more mature in their judgment. As the younger, more hot-headed men saw the example of their elder brethren, they realised that despite their younger years, they, too, were guilty of sin and felt the teaching of the new Rabbi sink deeper into their hearts. They walked away and left Jesus alone with the woman, although other crowds were now drawing in.

What would have happened to the judgment and reasoning power of the men if Jesus had made his statement straightaway? Would some of the younger men have cast their stones? A pause was needed, just like the tempering of the clay. Time was made so that Jesus could mould them with his words. By inserting time and a distraction, the men lost some of their fire and tempered down their actions. Jesus had the people demonstrate the principle of temperance by stealth. '*Blessed are the merciful, for they shall obtain mercy*'.

Jesus gave us many lessons, but perhaps the greatest was that he was willing to die so that those who don't deserve mercy can receive it. We, therefore, must look to that great lesson to forgive others rather than seek retribution. Vengeance belongs to God, and he will repay, but for us, it is required to forgive all men. The parable of a king who took account of his servants is an example of how Jesus can forgive, but if we don't forgive others, he can take that forgiveness back [Matthew 18:23-35].

Forgiveness vs Trust

Forgiveness is not the same as trust, and neither is love. Just because you love and forgive someone, you do not have to trust them. A person who has suffered abuse in any form may eventually have power given to help them forgive, but trust is earned. As discussed in this book, one can rightly be forgiven by God but not trusted to be a ruler in His kingdom. In the same way, one can rightly forgive another but not trust them to be a ruler in their house. These decisions should be made with fervent prayer and honesty to oneself and God. Being a Christian does not mean you have to be a victim.

The dictionary defines marriage as a contract by which two parties pledge to live together in mutual affection and fidelity. God's ideal of marriage is a covenant between a man and a woman, where two become united as though they were one flesh [Matthew 19:5-6+9]. It is a positive partnership where the expression of love also helps to replenish the earth. The woman is equal to the husband and protected by his virtue. Marriage was never meant to be a subservient entrapment. To say 'I do' is synonymous with 'I trust'.

Quick aside: *The other day, I listened to a Pink Floyd song called 'Another Brick in the Wall, Pt.2' which ends by cutting to an unhinged father shouting at his children as follows, 'If you don't eat your meat, you can't have any pudding, how can you have any pudding if you don't eat your meat!' His tone of voice is terrifying for a young child, but the angry parent would never have used the same tone for a friend who came to dinner and would probably appear so kind at church. It is the display of a* *father who is frustrated with his life decisions or circumstances and then vents that frustration on his family. The power of our words and the intonation in our voices will be recorded by angels and submitted as evidence of our character on the last day. If you struggle to control your tongue (which lives in a slippery place), then play the song and listen to the father at the end ranting at his children, imagining you are the child. This heart-wrenching debacle of fatherhood will change your soul if you allow it to. If this is something you have done in any way, take the opportunity to ask your family for forgiveness and repent to your Father in Heaven that you have offended his little ones [Luke 17:1-3]. Aiden Paul taught me that a father who rules with an iron fist will have no authority when the children leave the nest, while a father who rules with a glove of love will forever be a father to his children.*

To review:

- Take time to let a situation distil upon you, just as the clay must sit for a while to be tempered before it is put into action.
- A person can accidentally be a religious extremist, so remember that the fruit of the Spirit is love, peace, longsuffering, gentleness, meekness, and temperance.
- A person can defend themselves, but not at any expense. The innocent must be protected from our actions, and our actions must be proportionate to the threat.
- If you must make a point, make sure the doves are not turned over.

Simply put, we control what goes in and out of our body, including our words and actions [Matthew 15:17-20]. If you ever need to chastise someone, make sure you are willing to show love to them afterwards, just as Jesus did for the money changers one week later.

With all the power he had to descend from the cross and strike his crucifiers down for shedding innocent blood, Jesus showed ultimate control of his body and spirit by calling down forgiveness for his crucifiers rather than retribution. That was temperance.

PATIENCE

(James 1:4)

While temperance holds back natural urges, patience steadfastly works towards our spiritual urges. We might want our children or students to know twenty-five New Testament quotes word for word, have the personal stamina to run a marathon, or become a black belt in martial arts. All these are reasonable, lofty goals, but we should remember that perfection comes one drop of spiritual dew at a time. A person cannot make a wheat field ripen from seed in a day, so the spiritual harvest we seek will take a while. Many noble and lofty pursuits involve this element of time, which must pass before achieving the goal.

More than waiting, patience is an involved action. Simply watching TV while our crops grow is not patience. The actions required to bring a righteous harvest involve engagement with the desired result, such as fertilising the soil, protecting it with nets, watering, draining, walking the fields, and so forth. A person may have the time to serve their fellow man or develop a talent but not have the patience to do it. Each drop of water on a plant is needed, and many drops will be required, but throwing buckets of water sporadically will result in a drowned crop with negative outcomes.

I am currently learning to play my favourite tune on the piano. While I have no musical training, I can still follow instructions from tutorial videos to accomplish my goal.

The piano sits in the middle of the house, so I pass it often. Over the last three weeks, I have sat down each day to learn the next few notes in the tune while repeating the old notes I previously learned. Some of the tricky parts of the music are at the end, but I decided to approach the notes from the perspective of putting one foot in front of the other and not worry about how long it takes. Each day, I sit down for 5 to 10 minutes and build on what I know, so much so that I can now play the Hans Zimmer tune all the way through, with a few fancy bits I added of my own. Patience has brought forth the fruit of a tune in me.

Often, we have children, family or friends who do not want to know about the Gospel or are antagonistic towards it. Once again, patience is not ignoring the situation and gritting our teeth. Instead, patience involves pondering and praying about how we can help someone and then setting about our desire, knowing there is no time limit for the fruits of our labour to be realised. We can talk about our concerns with them, but equally, they may not want to hear. In this case, simply loving our neighbour as ourselves is enough. Maintaining a healthy relationship with someone, whereby they can see our lives and influence, might be enough to help them without a single word being spoken. Let your life be a window to the Saviour's love, so when they see you, they will see him. A person at our church had a seminary teacher who taught them, '*Watch your actions. You may be the only scripture somebody reads*', which reminds me of Francis Assisi's teaching, '*Only if it's necessary, use words.*'

Physical

I speak here from a position of weakness as I have not had to endure any long-term illness. I pray for those who suffer in this way and don't pretend to know how they feel.

People experience various physical ailments, and you might be dealing with one yourself. While this experience may help strengthen your spirit in unknown ways, it could also foster spiritual growth in your friends or family. An example is the story of the man with paralysis who was lowered through the roof into the house where Jesus was preaching [Mark 2:4]. Jesus saw the faith of those who brought their friend to be healed and they saw that his sins were forgiven. What lesson did his friends take away? Their faith was undoubtedly strengthened by seeing the fruits of their labour, but without the sick man, there would be no need to see the Saviour that day.

We have been strengthened by seeing the faith of people in scripture who were healed from long-term illnesses. They have suffered for years so that we might gain our faith. Will the years of suffering you or a friend have endured serve to bring you both closer to God, or to each other?

We suffer for many reasons, and our heartfelt yearnings for healing are not always met in our desired time frame. Paul seemed to have endured an ailment that the Lord would not heal.

'*And lest I should be exalted above measure through the abundance of the revelations, there was given to me a thorn in the flesh, the messenger of Satan to buffet me, lest I should be exalted above measure. For this thing I besought the Lord thrice, that it might depart from me. And he said unto me, My grace is sufficient for thee: for my strength is made perfect in weakness. Most gladly therefore will I rather glory in my infirmities, that the power of Christ may rest upon me. Therefore I take pleasure in infirmities, in reproaches, in necessities, in persecutions, in distresses for Christ's sake: for when I am weak, then am I strong.*'[2 Corinthians 12:7-10].

Through the enabling grace of the Lord Jesus Christ, our weaknesses can become our strengths. We had everything we needed in the Garden of Eden; therefore, we could not grow and improve. The struggles we face each day teach us what we need to know to become strong enough to climb the rock of Christ.

Patience does not mean suffering in silence, as we are encouraged to do everything we can to be healed. The woman who suffered from an issue of blood for twelve years had spent all her living on doctors before the Saviour healed her. The lame man at the pool of Bethesda had waited thirty-eight years to be healed, yet he still positioned himself at the pool in hope. Both of these people acted in faith. Imagine if the person who had been ill for 38 years had died one year before Christ's coming. That means he would have been released from suffering one year earlier. Whether liberated from suffering through death or healing, we can be strengthened to endure with patience. Job's immortal words come to mind, '*Naked came I out of my mother's womb, and naked shall I return thither: the Lord gave, and the Lord hath taken away; blessed be the name of the Lord.*'

Endurance

In James 5:11, we encounter the well-known phrase, '*the patience of Job*'. The root word for patience here in the KJV is elsewhere translated as 'endure'. The Greek word used is *hypomonen*, which means endurance and steadfastness. I find the word *steadfastness* particularly comforting. With the strength of God's grace, we can be steadfast in our trials, not giving up, but steadily moving forward, even if it's at a slow pace, like in a traffic jam, with a steadfastness in Christ. Fuelled by hope, our endurance will lead us back to our heavenly home, where all the sons of God will rejoice at our return, just as they rejoiced when the earth's foundations were laid [Job 38:4-7]. This promise of joy in our heavenly home should bring comfort and reassurance during our trials.

So, patience enables us to have peace—and even rejoice—when we diligently strive to accomplish the work the Lord has for us. With patience inside our souls, we can press forward, having a perfect brightness of hope, no matter how long it takes. If we die before our journeys through, then happy is the day for us, even though we do feel sadness for loved ones left behind.

The End Harvest

Patient Christian discipleship is the only path to perfection, distilling at a pace of a few spiritual dew drops each day. In time, perhaps at the end of the millennium or further, we will become pure as he is pure and righteous as he is righteous, or in other words, we can patiently refine our characters until we become like him and feel comfortable sitting at his table [1 John 3:2-7]. Jesus is our great exemplar of patiently enduring suffering and other afflictions. He counselled us to do the same with a cheerful heart, looking forward to a brighter future,

'*Blessed are they which are persecuted for righteousness' sake: for theirs is the kingdom of heaven. Blessed are ye, when men shall revile you, and persecute you, and shall say all manner of evil against you falsely, for my sake. Rejoice, and be exceeding glad: for great is your reward in heaven: for so persecuted they the prophets which were before you.*' [Matthew 5:10-12]

The end fruit of your harvest is a Christlike nature, and Jesus often refers to the reward for cultivating this fruit inside you as a place in his kingdom. It is not wrong to hope for a seat at his table with our family, as this motivation will help us endure all trials. Once more, it is only through the atonement of Jesus that we can have this hope.

The Comforter cannot comfort someone who is already comfortable [John 14:26-27].

One cannot enter into God's rest when they are already resting [Hebrews 4:8-11].

Four scriptures will round off the principle of patience here.

'*My brethren, count it all joy when ye fall into divers temptations; Knowing this, that the trying of your faith worketh* ***patience****. But let* ***patience*** *have her perfect work, that ye may be perfect and entire, wanting nothing.*' [James 1:2-5]

' *... which in an honest and good heart, having heard the word, keep it, and bring forth fruit with* ***patience****.*' [Luke 8:14-15]

'*For whatsoever things were written aforetime were written for our learning, that we through* ***patience*** *and comfort of the scriptures might have* ***hope****. Now the God of* ***patience*** *and consolation grant you to be likeminded one toward another according to Christ Jesus*' [Romans 15:4-5]

'*... but we glory in tribulations also: knowing that tribulation worketh* ***patience****; and* ***patience****, experience; and experience,* ***hope***' [Romans 5:3-4]

Patience is peacefully and purposefully working towards the harvest we hope for, no matter how long it takes.

BROTHERLY KINDNESS

(Philippians 2:2)

The attribute of kindness perfectly encapsulates the Gospel of Jesus Christ and is the very soil from which Christians are grown. My favourite quote is by Ella's mother in the 2015 film Cinderella, just before she died. '*Ella, my darling, I want to tell you a secret, a great secret that will see you through all the trials that life can offer. You must always remember this ... have courage and be kind.*'

Kind is the kind of people we are to be.

Kindliness

The etymology of the word is fascinating. In Greek, the word for Kindness comes from *Chrestos* (5543 Χρηστος), which means good, useful, gentle and pleasant. The Greek words for Christ and Kindness are so closely related that if you spoke the Greek word for *Christ* the Anointed (5547 Χριστος), it would sound the same as the word for Kindness.

Never has a kinder or gentler man walked the face of the earth than Jesus. The words 'kindness' and 'merciful' are interchangeable, as you cannot express one without the other. Just as Jesus said in the sermon on the mount, '*blessed are the merciful: for they shall obtain mercy*', so you could also pen '*blessed are the kind: for they shall obtain kindness.*' Being kind to your kin is easier than your enemy, but we are still commanded to love and pray for our enemies [Matthew 5:43-44]. Having kindness towards an enemy is a 'choice' we first make before it becomes an 'attribute' we have [Psalm 117].

In Part I, Chapter Five, you may remember a discussion on the Hebrew word *hesed* which covers the same principles discussed with Brotherly Kindness. Around this point, the fractals of Godliness begin to blend into each other, so we will see some overlap, especially as we get closer to the capstone of Christ's characteristics Igloo.

Brotherly

While the term *brother* can refer to your blood brother or your brother in the faith, I cannot help but hear the question from Luke 10, when a particular lawyer asked Jesus, '*Who is my neighbour?*' to which Jesus replied by giving the parable of the Good Samaritan. Jesus broadened the definition of a neighbour to include any of the human family. The gospel of Jesus Christ was not limited in scope to the Jews or even Israel but to all humanity. Hence, our brother is the same as our neighbour in God's eyes.

Perhaps Peter used the term '*brotherly kindness*' rather than just '*kindness*' because it gives context to help us achieve the desired result. Knowing all mankind should be treated as our brother or sister helps us understand how we should act towards one another. A wicked man who tries to become kind can take his knowledge of how to treat his family and extend that action to other people. It should be remembered that we are all genuinely the children of God, and hence, we are all genuinely brothers and sisters in Christ.

David, who slew Goliath, had a best friend in Saul's son, Johnathan. They enjoyed a bond as close as blood brothers, but David's relationship with Johnathan's father was rocky and deadly. Despite the threats to his life, David would not kill Saul when he had the chance. Between Johnathan and Saul, we see the two extremes of brotherly kindness exhibited, as David extended mercy to his enemy Saul in the cave [1 Samuel 24], and Johnathan extended unlimited kindness to David throughout all his generations in the future,

'*Then said Jonathan unto David, Whatsoever thy soul desireth, I will even do it for thee ... Go in peace, forasmuch as we have sworn both of us in the name of the Lord, saying, The Lord be between me and thee, and between my seed and thy seed for ever.*' [1 Samuel 20:4 + 42]. Mizpah [Genesis 31:49]

Ruth and Naomi show a bond as though they were blood relations. Naomi released Ruth from looking after her after the death of her son, to whom Ruth was married, yet Ruth replied with the epithet '*whither thou goest, I will go; and where thou lodgest, I will lodge: thy people shall be my people, and thy God my God*' [Ruth 1:16].

Life was not a bed of roses among the early church missionaries. Paul's refusal to go with Mark on a missionary journey due to his previous neglect of duty is an example of contention, which is the antithesis of what we are talking about [Acts 15]. A little extra kindness—mixed with mercy—could have helped on this occasion. Thankfully, the rift appears to have healed over time [2 Timothy 4:11].

Later on, in Paul's letter to the Philippians, he writes

'*[be] of one accord, of one mind. Let nothing be done through strife or vainglory; but in lowliness of mind let each esteem [each]other better than themselves. Look not every man on his own things, but every man also on the things of others. Let this mind be in you, which was also in Christ Jesus*' [Philippians 2:1-5].

The commandment that we love our neighbour as ourselves is the second greatest, yet the attribute of kindness here suggests we love our brother above ourselves, where he says, '*let each esteem [each]other better than themselves*'. Jesus explained this new commandment at the Last Supper, which we will discuss later under the attribute of charity, but for now, remember that brotherly kindness is not limited by law, but is striven for by those who seek a Zion society where all are of one heart and one mind. Indeed, a Zion society will be kind to each other, and hence, the kingdom of God can be among us now if we adopt this attitude towards our neighbours [Luke 17:21; Acts 4:31-32].

Quick aside: *KJV translates Luke 17:21 as 'Neither shall they say, Lo here! or, lo there! for, behold, the kingdom of God is within you.' But other translations suggest it should read '... the kingdom of God is in your midst', or 'among you'. Hence, we can create Zion on earth among us, should we choose his way of life.*

Opposite

The opposite of Brotherly Kindness is expressed after Cain killed Abel in the book of Genesis.

'*And the Lord said unto Cain, Where is Abel thy brother? And he said, I know not: Am I my brother's keeper?*' [Genesis 4:9]

While we all know murder is wrong, it is the dismissal of murder by the phrase '*Am I my brother's keeper?*' which has lived in infamy throughout the centuries. How often has that same sentiment been expressed by those who seek to justify their neglect of unwritten duty towards their fellow man?

Jesus enhanced the commandment '*Thou shalt not kill*' to become a more excellent principle.

'*whosoever is angry with his brother ... shall be in danger of the judgment: and whosoever shall say to his brother, Raca [stupid air-head], shall be in danger of the council: but whosoever shall say, Thou fool, shall be in danger of hell fire*' [Matthew 5:22].

We are our brother's keeper, insomuch that we are to be mindful of our neighbour, as in the case of the good

Samaritan. Satan—that old serpent—would have us be angry, call each other derogatory names, and thereby devolve ourselves of unity and kindness.

I recently spoke with a couple of truckers who take helicopters to different parts of the country for repair. They commented on the local McDonald's restaurant, suggesting it was more like a community care centre. All the staff they encountered were genuinely helpful and went beyond their call of duty. One staff member was chatting with a lone older gentleman sitting in the corner, asking about his week. The greeter approached them during their meal and was genuinely interested in how they were, and as they left, the person sweeping the car park looked up and wished them a pleasant evening. They may not have been church members, but they were ready for a Zion society. If the Kingdom of God were to descend in glory upon Norwich, I hazard to say that the angels, although more potent in their ability to move and see, would not be any more pleasant and kind than those staff working at McDonald's.

The Home

One purpose of our lives here on earth is to demonstrate to God we can be trusted so he can make us rulers in his kingdom, knowing we would always use his power for good, not selfish designs. The greatest power he gives us while here on the earth is to create life and join with him (to some degree) as co-creators. The home can become a source of contention and strife if we allow it to be, but peace is achieved through our kind and forgiving choices.

As parents, we should exemplify this behaviour with our spouse and children, who mimic us. In the home, we learn brotherly kindness; from home, we change the world.

My mother passed away when I was a teenager, and one strong recollection I have of that time is when her friend told me what she admired most about my mum. Whenever she heard of someone else's success, she would say in her Welsh accent, '*There's lovely*' and genuinely mean it. She did not suffer from brotherly jealousy even though she had difficulties which I have never had to bear. She took joy from the success of others and taught me to avoid narrowly judging people, criticizing them, or saying negative things about them.

In so many ways, I am grateful to my mum, who exemplified kindness x

'*And be ye kind one to another, tender-hearted, forgiving one another, even as God for Christ's sake hath forgiven you.*' [Ephesians 4:32]

GODLINESS

(Isaiah 52:11)

When I was a lad, the phrase often spoken by adults was '*Cleanliness is next to Godliness*'. I genuinely feel this is true. The term 'reverence', or 'piety', denotes the attitude of someone who is in awe of someone else. Naturally, one would be in awe of God if he appeared to us, as he has to people in the past. Moses was told to remove the shoes from his feet, and Peter, James, and John wanted to make booths (tents) for the heavenly beings on the Mount of Transfiguration. If you knew God was going to show up at your house tomorrow, I am sure your home would be swept clean and made spick 'n' span for his arrival. You would do this because you reverence his name rather than being commanded to clean up.

We have a friend coming over from America to stay with us next week, and this visit led to me being outside for three days, jet-washing the patio blocks and digging out wasteland to lay down limestone chippings in an effort to tidy the place up. These things needed doing anyway, but knowing our friend was coming helped motivate us to get on and be ready.

When you consider your life, there may be many things you could improve, which can easily be upgraded; probably things you have known for a long time needed doing. If you desire clarification on what these things are, ask your best friend or your spouse. If you are really brave, ask your children :0)

We attend church in our Sunday best to show God we are willing to do our best for Him. There is no laughter nor idle speech when we partake of the emblems of his body and blood. We look inward, committing to improving this week the areas which the Spirit whispers to our souls we need to work on, just like I knew I had to work on the garden to get it in shape. We all have weeds to remove and areas to improve.

Perhaps your life before becoming a Christian (or even after) was like a derelict building which needed a complete revamp. If so, there would be debris scattered around which would hinder converting your house into the palace spoken of by C. S. Lewis. The act of clearing up your building site, removing broken bricks and uprooting dead trees is an act of godliness. Whether someone is clearing their lands of sin or is fully clear already, both are godly people.

The Greek word for '*godly*' reflects reverence and a religious life. Just as we have birthdays to remember our family and friends, we have ceremonies to keep God in mind, such as the sacramental bread. When a person is baptised, they become symbolically clean, which cleanliness is next to godliness. When people partake of the bread and wine, they actively remember the covenant they made to take up their cross and follow him, which strengthens their bond with God. Every action which moves us closer to him is an act of godliness.

Paul listed some aspects of godliness in his letter to Titus,

'... exhort to be sober minded. In all things shewing thyself a pattern of good works: in doctrine shewing uncorruptness, gravity, sincerity, sound speech, that cannot be condemned; that he that is of the contrary part may be ashamed, having no evil thing to say of you ... For the grace of God that bringeth salvation hath appeared to all men, teaching us that, <u>denying ungodliness and worldly lusts,</u> we should live soberly, righteously, and godly, in this present world ...' [Titus 2:6-12].

Extracting from the text those words which help remove ungodliness we have:

- Soberness
- Good works
- Uncorruption
- Gravity
- Sincerity
- Sound speech
- Righteousness

Effectively, these aspects of godliness put a person beyond reproach, insomuch that an enemy would have nothing evil to say about them. Jesus exemplified sound speech by saying nothing when brought before the high priest. In this world, the adversary can try to trip us up in many ways, such that, in a moment of pride, we can teach true doctrine as though it were a venomous barb. Sometimes, we act godly by keeping quiet.

Paul counsels us to be godly by gently teaching true doctrine and being content with what we have. He said the ungodly person would have pride, envy and argue about the doctrine of Christ [1 Timothy 6:3-6].

In the Beatitudes, we are counselled to be peacemakers, which is a godly act.

Quick aside: *The city of Jerusalem means, the 'dwelling of peace', as salem means 'peace' in Hebrew. It will also be a future city in heaven, where the godly will dwell, as every kingdom has a law and those who are obedient to the law of the city are allowed to live there. Compliance with the laws of Gods kingdom is known as 'godliness'.*

The opposite of godliness is '*licentiousness*', which denotes someone who has no principles to govern their actions, disregards the rules of society, and thereby moves further away from God. For example, we British have a reputation for queuing respectfully in line, as a mark of our 'Britishness'. A licentious person would choose to push in as they have no moral restraint. So it is that a *godly* person would desire to abide by the rules of a heavenly society as a mark of their 'Godliness'. Most of our libraries are free to enter, but there is a rule that we speak quietly in them. If a person chooses to shout, they will be chastised or escorted out, even though entrance is free to all.

Another sign of good manners is saying 'Excuse me' or 'Pardon me' when we make a mistake. The Psalmist brings this request for repentance into the notion of godliness when he says,

'I acknowledged my sin unto thee, and mine iniquity have I not hid. I said, I will confess my transgressions unto the Lord; and thou forgavest the iniquity of my sin ... For this shall every one that is godly pray unto thee in a time when thou mayest be found: surely in the floods of great waters they shall not come nigh unto him.' [Psalm 32:5-6]

Here, we are reminded that a godly person will pray for forgiveness before the last day when the floods come, and he is drowning in the sea of sin. The Psalmist's historical reference was Noah's flood, but in New Testament times, we speak of the day of burning, when the elements will melt with fervent heat [2 Peter 3:12]. The time to repent is before these calamities come upon us, which is what a godly person would do as they want to be clean. **It is the godly who repent each day, not the sinners.**

In researching, I discovered that Jude is my favourite writer on the subject. Along with James, Jude was a half-brother of Jesus, but his journey towards godliness probably started after the crucifixion. One thing really frustrated him ... the ungodly men who turned the grace of Jesus Christ into an excuse for lasciviousness and licentiousness. Hell has two L's in its name, which are the initials of these two descriptive words. As a comparison, Jude brings into remembrance the epoch-defining moment of God delivering the children of Israel from Egypt. In the quote below, all the people were saved from Egypt, but none made it to the promised land, save Caleb and Joshua. Jude wants us to remember that false grace is teaching others they can be lawless, lack moral restraints, and disregard the rules simply due to the grace of God. Being saved once from Egypt (the world) does not guarantee salvation in the promised land (heaven), as shown below by Jude.

'*For there are certain men crept in unawares, who were before of old ordained to this condemnation, ungodly men, turning the grace of our God into lasciviousness, and denying the only Lord God, and our Lord Jesus Christ. I will therefore put you in remembrance, though ye once knew this, how that the Lord, having saved the people out of the land of Egypt, afterward destroyed them that believed not ... clouds they are without water, carried about of winds; trees whose fruit withereth, without fruit, twice dead, plucked up by the roots'* [Jude 1:4-5+12].

The imagery of a cloud without water or a tree without fruit is poignant. The ungodly would turn the Gospel into an excuse for unbridled, dirty living, without order, without cleanliness.

Our house should be a house of prayer, a house of fasting, a house of faith, a house of learning, a house of glory, a house of order, a house of God. As we clean our kitchen each day and set our garden in order, let us look at our own lives and ask if the fruit we offer him at our table or altar is clean. Do we let our garden become overgrown with the notion that Jesus will do the gardening for us when he returns? Remember, Jesus removes waste and teaches how to prune, but you are the gardener [Matthew 21:33-41]. It is not requisite that a man should run faster than he has strength. If you have a small garden, you can keep it well-maintained in your sphere of influence, but remember that fake grass has no life, and fake trees produce no fruit [Mark 4:20].

As Isaiah taught, '*be ye clean, that bear the vessels of the Lord.*'

CHARITY

(1 Corinthians 13:13)

If you were to bake a celestial cake, the chiefest of all Christlike ingredients would be charity, a combination of all the colours in Christ's spectrum, providing clear, white light. Charity is not the icing on the cake of Christianity, but its very substance.

In his book, 'The Four Loves', C.S. Lewis explains that love can be categorized into four general types: familial, friendship, romantic, and unconditional love. The fourth type, unconditional love, is what charity refers to. The Greek word *Agape* (mentioned in Part I) signifies the deepest form of love, as described in John 3:16. This is the kind of love a parent feels for a child, but extends to others as well. While someone may feel empathy for a homeless man and be encouraged to give generously, this feeling does not reach the level of charity described by Agape.

I don't want to expound on this doctrine without first acknowledging the level of difficulty associated with it and my own inadequacy. We are talking about an attribute born deep down in the soil of compassion and rooted in the bowels of our souls [Ephesians 3:17]. This enduring love sustains us in our darkest depths; when hope seems lost, faith is held onto by fingertips, and other virtues hang by a thread. One day, we might find that every other attribute is nothing more than scaffolding to help us reach the pinnacle of this principle. Once attained, we find that charity is a pillar that stands tall, solid and true, firmly rooted and independent. Indeed, all principles, doctrines and commandments are designed to illuminate this one pillar as if they were but stage lights in the auditorium of charity.

One example from scripture that points to the level of love Jesus has for us is the shepherd and the sheep. Stop for a moment and consider ... A sheep is not human, but a shepherd is.

'*I am the good shepherd ... I lay down my life for the sheep*' [John 10:14-15]

You and I might consider laying down our lives for another human, and many have. The level of difference between an animal and a human might be the level of difference between a human and a God. While we love and care for animals, we would not lay down our lives for them. Would you sacrifice your child for a sheep? Of course not. Such a comparison highlights the condescension and deep-rooted love that God and Jesus have for us.

High-level charity is synonymous with high-level love and is much more than a charitable donation. The good Samaritan did not simply put money in a hat.

'Though I speak with the tongues of men and of angels, and have not charity, I am become as sounding brass, or a tinkling cymbal. And though I have the gift of prophecy, and understand all mysteries, and all knowledge; and though I have all faith, so that I could remove mountains, and have not charity, I am nothing. And though I bestow

all my goods to feed the poor, and though I give my body to be burned, and have not charity, it profiteth me nothing.' [1 Corinthians 13:1–3]

What Charity does:

- ✓ *suffers long*
- ✓ *is kind*
- ✓ *rejoices in the truth*
- ✓ *bears all things*
- ✓ *believes all things*
- ✓ *hopes all things*
- ✓ *endures all things*
- ✓ *never fail*

What Charity doesn't:

- *envieth not*
- *vaunts not itself*
- *is not puffed up*
- *doth not behave itself unseemly*
- *seeks not her own*
- *is not easily provoked*
- *thinks no evil*
- *rejoices not in iniquity*

[1 Corinthians 13:4–13]

All attributes and commandments can be broken down into an element of charity. In the end, there are only two great commandments, and both involve this type of love. Conversely, we see that Pride, in all its forms, is the antithesis of Charity.

In his letter to Timothy, Paul states, '*Now the end of the commandment is charity'*, highlighting how it is in the DNA of all the commandments [1 Timothy 1:5].

Rules, order, and structure are necessary parts of God's Kingdom on earth, but once the bullet has left the gun, its trajectory is the only thing that matters. When our life on earth is complete, and all the children stand to be judged, it is the trajectory we are on which will determine the type of resurrection we are allocated, be it the *sun, moon* or *stars* [1 Corinthians 15:41-42]. As mentioned before, 'sin' means falling short of a target. Charity is the trajectory which never fails.

Peter tells us that charity has a unique function,

'*... the end of all things is at hand: be ye therefore sober, and watch unto prayer. And above all things have fervent charity among yourselves: for <u>charity shall cover</u> the multitude of sins*' [1 Peter 4:8].

We have already seen that the word 'atonement' means to 'cover'; therefore, charity has an element of redemption within its remit. Through charity, we help people 're-cover' from their lost and fallen state, whether physically or spiritually. We clothe them; we cover them. Only God can forgive people from their sins and admit them into heaven, but we can forgive a prodigal son and welcome them back into our home. When we extend the pure love of Christ through forgiving others, we have access to the redemption of Jesus Christ in our own lives. Jesus taught this principle in the parable of the King, which took an account of his servants in Matthew 18:23-35.

Along with covering sins, it would be proper to say that charity prevents a multitude of sins, insomuch that a person filled with charity would not sin against others because of his genuine love for them. We would not steal from, lie to, or kill someone we love, nor would a charitable person dishonour their parents even when they have not been the best. Being angry with someone is not a burden we must carry, as charity liberates us from anger. A person who has the love of God in their soul would never commit adultery with another man's wife nor think of such things in his mind's eye. Charity not only covers our sins, but much rather, it prevents them.

The Bond of Charity

Most dressing gowns have a belt, and many other outfits, including ancient robes, would have a belt known as a *'bond'* that ties everything together. Charity is the bond, girdle, or belt which holds your robe of righteousness together.

'*And above all these things put on charity, which is the bond of perfectness.*' [Colossians 3:14]

We know the five foolish virgins in Matthew 25 did not have enough oil in their lamps while they waited for the bridegroom to come, but what does the oil represent? We often correctly say it is our testimonies or our witness of Jesus Christ. Jesus gave additional guidance in Luke 12:33-43 where he counsels those who wait for him to have their loins '*girded about*', which means we should be found serving others when he comes again. If you can imagine trying to run in a long robe or dress, you could trip over the hem and fall flat on your face, so in ancient days, they would lift their robes and tuck them into their belts to avoid stumbling as they ran or worked. This is the meaning of the phrase '*Gird up your loins*', or in other words, '*Get stuck in!*'.

Charity keeps all the attributes of Christlikeness together, like a belt holding our trousers up or keeping our robes fastened. Without a belt, we would struggle to work. Without charity, we look like poorly dressed Christians, with many of our imperfections on display.

Dress for the Wedding

Many are called to the wedding feast on the last day, but not all who are bidden will come [Matthew 22:2-5]. Those who do come must be wearing a garment [Matthew 22:11-13]. Regarding the bride, she will be wearing fine white linen, which represents the righteousness of the saints,

'Let us be glad and rejoice, and give honour to him: for the marriage of the Lamb is come, and his wife hath made herself ready. And to her was granted that she should be arrayed in fine linen, clean and white: for the fine linen is the righteousness of saints.' [Revelation 19:5-10].

The word 'righteousness' used here is about the *righteous acts* of the sanctified people (*dikaióma* 1345) rather than the righteous acts of someone else. Thus, we see that the garment we wear should be presentable, and what better attribute is there to hold everything together than the bond of charity?

Those who attend the wedding but choose not to wear the garment will be thrown out, as the end of the parable reminds us,

'*Then said the king to the servants, Bind him hand and foot, and take him away, and cast him into outer darkness; there shall be weeping and gnashing of teeth. For many are called, but few are chosen.*' [Matthew 22:13-14]

Peter explains that to have our calling and election made sure, we must be wearing the attributes of Christ covered in Part II as taught in 2 Peter 1:5-8. He then encourages us as follows,

'*Wherefore the rather, brethren, give diligence to make your calling and election sure: for if ye do these things, ye shall never fall: For so an entrance shall be ministered unto you abundantly into the everlasting kingdom of our Lord and Saviour Jesus Christ.*' [2 Peter 1:10-11].

While we have all been called, many will refuse to attend the wedding, as shown in Matthew 22, or they might attend the wedding but refuse to wear the proper garment.

'*Many will say to me in that day, Lord, Lord, have we not prophesied in thy name? and in thy name have cast out devils? and in thy name done many wonderful works? And then will I profess unto them, I never knew you: depart from me*' [Matthew 7:22-24].

Jesus invites us to be appropriately dressed at the wedding when he comes again, clothed with the bond of charity.

A New Commandment

The synoptic gospels of Matthew, Mark, and Luke cover the Last Supper in just one chapter, and even then, only a few verses. John, however, dedicates a quarter of his book to the teachings of the Messiah during their final meal in the upper room, which some have equated to a graduation ceremony for his disciples. This was a pivotal event, a culmination of Jesus' mortal ministry. We could look at the Sermon on the Mount (in Matthew) and the Last Supper discourse (in John) as bookends which hold a great weight of doctrine. It was here in the upper room that Jesus issued a new commandment.

For background, when a lawyer asked, *'Master, which was the great commandment in the law*?' [Matthew 22:35], Jesus' answer became iconic and prefaced the parable of the good Samaritan (when viewed in Luke 10). His answer was given as follows:

1) Love God with all your heart, soul and mind
2) Love your neighbour as yourself.

The lawyer knew this, and Jesus congratulated him, as this was old-school law. However, just as Jesus enhanced the Ten Commandments during the Sermon on the Mount, he was about to enhance the second great commandment at the Last Supper. For those select disciples who were present, after he had washed their feet and dismissed Judas, Jesus began to teach,

'*A new commandment I give unto you, That ye love one another; as I have loved you, that ye also love one another*' [John 13:34].

Often, I glossed over the fact that the commandment to love one another '*as I have loved you*' is new. The Greek word translated as 'new' here is *kainen* (2537), which means fresh and unused; hence, we must consider what is fresh about it.

It comes in chiasmic form,

- *Love one another*
- ***As I have loved you***
- *Love one another*

The previous second greatest commandment was:

- *Love thy neighbour* ***as thyself***

The supernal shift is from loving your neighbour as though you represent yourself to loving your neighbour as though you represent Christ, acting as he would.

This teaching comes right off the back of Jesus washing his disciples' feet. Only a parent or a servant would wash your dirty feet or even touch your toes. A servant (hireling) would act out of necessity, whereas a parent (Jesus) acts out of love [John 10:11-12]. He wants us to love as he loves. Extending grace to others is the new commandment.

Grace: The Highest Form of Charity

During his mortal ministry, Jesus never used the word 'grace' yet exemplified it with his actions. After his death, the disciples encapsulated his life and teachings in this single word.

Luke refers to grace in passing about Jesus growing up,

'*And the child grew, and waxed strong in spirit, filled with wisdom: and the grace of God was upon him.*' [Luke 2:40]

Grace is more than a teaching of how we are saved from sin; it refers to the kind of love God shows to his Son, and the Son shows to us—the type of love that leaves a mark [Zachariah 13:6]. We are invited to show this same model of selfless love to others. God's grace was upon Jesus; Jesus' grace is upon us; our miming grace should be upon others. Remember, Jesus grew into perfection through his Father's enabling grace, and likewise, we grow into perfection through Jesus' enabling grace. As we show grace to others, they, too, look to Jesus.

Strong's H2580, H2581, G5485, G5486 & G5487 all refer to the substance known as grace, and they share the following descriptors: Favour, Gratitude, Blessing, Kindness, Forgiveness & Endowment.

Our grace for others reflects his love for us. Hence, we become the *light of the world* in the same way the moon is the *light of the world* through its reflection of the sun. When we emulate the Saviour, we comfort those in darkness. First, we need Jesus' grace to forgive us of our sins, and second, we need Jesus' grace to help us forgive others, as it is not natural to forgive. Jesus forgives our debts so we can be saved; therefore, as etched into the Lord's Prayer, we cannot continue in our saved condition without forgiving others their debts as well.

When we forgive others, we are demonstrating charity, of which there are several levels, the highest of all being a manifestation of his grace. To attain grace, one must pray for a pure heart and be willing to practice loving others until it becomes a genuine part of their nature.

Level 1) Giving money to the beaten-up Jew
Level 2) Taking him in
Level 3) Forgiving the Robber

Bringing the end back to the beginning, in the Sermon on the Mount, Jesus said,

'*Blessed are the pure in heart: for **they shall see God***'.

It is the privilege of those who have purified (sanctified) themselves through the atonement of Jesus Christ to be brought back into the presence of God.

'we know that, when he shall appear, we shall be like him; for we shall see him as he is. And every man that hath this hope in him purifieth himself, even as he is pure.' [1 John 3:2-3; 1 Peter 1:16; Matthew 11:27]

'He that hath my commandments, and keepeth them, he it is that loveth me ... and I will love him, and will manifest myself to him.' [John 14:21; Hebrews 12:14]

Of all the gifts of the spirit, charity is the one we should pray for with all the energy of our hearts. There may be specific aspects of it we are struggling with, so praying for those particular things will be most worthwhile to us, but if you are just starting and recognise the need to develop this kind of love, then pray fervently for charity with all diligence, as '*The effectual fervent prayer of a righteous man availeth much*' [James 5:16].

Conclusion

The Lord saves us by his infinite grace, as we strive to save others by our lesser grace. When we have the power to feed the hungry, we should provide for them; when someone is naked, we should clothe them; if someone desires forgiveness, we should forgive them.

'*And of his fullness have all we received, and grace for grace.*' [John 1:16]

We will close this section on charity with Jesus' words from the sermon on the mount.

'*Ye have heard that it hath been said, Thou shalt love thy neighbour, and hate thine enemy. But I say unto you, Love your enemies, bless them that curse you, do good to them that hate you, and pray for them which despitefully use you, and persecute you; That ye may be the children of your Father which is in heaven ... Be ye therefore perfect, even as your Father which is in heaven is perfect.*'

This is the way of truth

End note

Part II is complete; I encourage you to write in your journal the trials you face as you follow the way of truth; record how you have overcome them and intend to hold on. Write the feelings in your heart towards your Father in heaven and record other things which stir your soul. This book serves as a journal to my children—the sand and the dust—sharing with them the lessons learned as I climb. On my shelf at home sit many other journals, each containing a part of my journey. Let your life lessons become mini-scriptures of faith to bless your posterity, whether born or unborn, helping to keep them continually in the right way. Let them remember that their forbearers knew the difficulty of the course, yet they finished the race firm in the faith.

After listing Christ's attributes, Peter said, '*For if these things be in you, and abound, they make you that ye shall neither be barren nor unfruitful in the knowledge of our Lord Jesus Christ. But he that lacketh these things is blind, and cannot see afar off, and hath forgotten that he was purged from his old sins. Wherefore the rather, brethren, give diligence to make your calling and election sure: for if ye do these things, ye shall never fall:* ***For so an entrance shall be ministered unto you abundantly into the everlasting kingdom*** *of our Lord and Saviour Jesus Christ. Wherefore I will not be negligent to put you always in remembrance of these things*' [2 Peter 1:8-12].

Please note that there is a qualifier to prevent us from falling, which I have underlined. While we practice climbing during this life, falling often, the goal is to become like the Free Soloist who never fell. Over time, the way to become like him is to practice these attributes. If one becomes so practised, when they have been tried and tested in all things and proved faithful, they will find their calling and election made sure, whereas until now, their election is conditional, as with all Israel. There is a difference between being saved from your *falls* and having an entrance ministered unto you in the everlasting kingdom of the Lord, when you are holding on so tightly to the attributes of Christ that you '*never fall*' again. This is your calling and election. Hence, many are called but few are chosen at the wedding [Matthew 22:14].

We can only finish something we have started; today is the day of our probation. Begin at Alpha and end with Omega.

May you press forward equally yoked with Christ [Matthew 11:29], ploughing the field of life, not looking back [Luke 9:62]. Sow seeds of faith for generations to come and make your calling and election sure.

Perhaps before continuing to the supplements, maybe take a moment to go back and read the section '**Where We Started**' at the beginning of the book to see if T. S. Eliot's quote was appropriate and if the principle of 'Grace for Grace' sits peacefully within you.

The Alpha scripture in this book is John 1:16

The Omega scripture is John 15:10-12

Our <u>fullness</u> of joy comes by

mirroring Grace.

Captain's Log: Supplemental

Fortitude

'*And Jesus said unto him, No man, having put his hand to the plough, and looking back, is fit for the kingdom of God.*' [Luke 9:62]

As a young, lapsed Protestant with no idea what I should be protesting about, my sister introduced me to the Douglas Adams book 'Hitchhikers Guide to the Galaxy', which became my bible. It was super funny, and I loved space, so it ticked my boxes.

In the book, a group of hyper-intelligent beings ask a supercomputer known as 'Deep Thought' the answer to the ultimate question of life, the universe, and everything. The supercomputer took 7.5 million years to come up with an answer, 42, but pointed out they needed to design a much bigger computer to determine the ultimate question. The name of this bigger computer was 'Earth'.

Recognising Douglas Adams didn't have a genuine reason for choosing 42, he may have done an *Arthur Dent* and stumbled on the correct answer without realising, but simply mispronounced it. Rather than 'forty-two', perhaps the answer was 'fortitude', and here's why ...

The Webster 1828 dictionary defines fortitude as '*That strength or firmness of mind or soul which enables a person to encounter danger with coolness and courage, or to bear pain or adversity without murmuring, depression or despondency ... Fortitude is the guard and support of the other virtues*'.

It is crucial to guard the virtues discussed in Part II, so we don't become lax or lazy in using them. We strive not to allow frustration, pain, or adversity to cause us to murmur, be depressed, or lose our cool. These ten attributes can be likened to pearls of great price. Pearls are formed when an irritant gets into an oyster's shell and causes it to secrete a substance over it. The substance of fortitude we secrete over our daily irritants enables Christlike virtues to be developed, preserved, and perfected. Once we know about the ten, it is vital that we recognize our weaknesses and diligently work on them until they are transformed into pearls.

My eldest was a socially apprehensive child and continues to prefer non-social time as any 'ISFJ' would, yet growing up in a church environment has enabled her perceived weakness to become a strength when she wants it to be. She served as a missionary on the other side of the world in Chile, led groups of youth from combined churches and addressed conferences in the UK & South Korea. Many micro opportunities for service in the church, which could be considered irritants, have helped her grow into a confident and effective leader on a larger scale, even though she would temporarily be happier curled up on the sofa with Boycee, the dog.

This process of growth reminds me of another quote by Neil A. Maxwell, '*God does not begin by asking our ability, only our availability, and if we prove our dependability, He will increase our capability.*'

Indeed, this is true, for I have seen it in many who come to our table and share in our lives. The gospel of Jesus Christ helps us become pearls rather than clam up in so many ways. The Lord will help turn our weaknesses into strengths as we secrete the pearlescent substance of fortitude over our trials and troubles.

As fellow travellers on earth, we have addressed those attributes we are expected to learn and practice, none of which are irrelevant or superfluous to a Christian. We are to be tried and tested on every level. God will not suffer us to be tempted or tried above our ability to endure, even though some trials are seemingly impossible to bear.

Jesus said,

'For whosoever will save his life shall lose it: and whosoever will lose his life for my sake shall find it.' [Matthew 16:24-25]

We are unaware of the reason for all our suffering, and not all trials are instigated by God, but he can certainly turn our sufferings around so that nothing we endure is wasted. A broken piece of steel, welded together, is often more robust than before. The Japanese practice of Kintsugi—where cracked and broken bowls are mended with gold—is true in our lives. If broken, we can become better versions of ourselves when repaired by God. One missionary I know was an excellent dancer who broke her legs during a pivotal audition. As she nursed her fractured body and considered the lost opportunities, she did not curse God and die as Job's wife told him to do [Job 2:9], but saw God's hand and felt impressed to take another course in life. She became a full-time missionary and now invites people to come unto Christ. The worth of souls is great in the sight of God, and if we should labour all our days to bring but one soul unto him, how great shall be our joy with them in the kingdom of our Father. [to Eva]

If you are broken, let the atonement of Jesus Christ put you back together in newer and holier ways.

Some of the blessings we desire are based upon our faith being tested to its limits, as was Abraham. We could pray for answers over many decades, such as Sariah, who was 90 years old before her promised blessing of being a 'mother of nations' began to be realised. Leah, Rachel, and Hannah struggled to have children, so their faith was stretched. Sadly, some women remain childless throughout their lives.

When righteously desired blessings are withheld, there can be a mistaken notion that this is due to unrighteousness. In the time of Jesus, a person was born blind, and the assumption was that either they or their parents had sinned for such a thing to happen. Jesus dispelled this thought, showing that suffering is not always a result of sin. We should not be hard on ourselves when our desired blessings do not come to pass. It is mostly God's will to try us rather than punish us, for we must be refined as silver and purified as gold [Proverbs 17:3, Job 23:10]. The fiery furnace is hot and burns for a reason. We cannot expect an easy ride through life, but this is not because of sin or unworthiness. The life of Job demonstrates fortitude to the Nth degree. We pass through trials to become more fit for the kingdom.

'*Beloved, think it not strange concerning the fiery trial which is to try you, as though some strange thing happened unto you: But rejoice, inasmuch as ye are partakers of Christ's sufferings; that, when his glory shall be revealed, ye may be glad also with exceeding joy.*' [1 Peter 4:12-13]

God loves us too much to take away all our trials, for our adolescent attributes reach maturity within them.

We know that each person must enter the kingdom—which will come down from heaven—through a gate made of a single pearl [Revelation 21:21; 22:14]. This represents to me how all the truths & attributes of Christ can be rolled into one great whole within us, enabling us to enter into his presence, shining with pearlescent light. Just as with Job, some people's burdens can seem too much to bear, yet they can be met with unwavering faith no matter the outcome in our lifetimes. The answer to overcoming these difficulties and struggles, which form pearls of great price within us, is to pray for and practice *forty-two.*

40 Kingdom Requirements

The following tables discuss the citizenship rules of God's Kingdom, also known as the Kingdom of Heaven, Salvation and Eternal Life. There would be no need for a ruler if there were no rules.

The number of requirements listed may seem daunting, but please keep in mind that you are already doing the majority of these things to a greater or lesser extent.

Jesus taught Nicodemus that to **enter** the kingdom of God, one must be born of the Spirit. No child born of the Spirit is meant to remain in spiritual infancy; instead, they are to mature into the fullness of Christ. Only those born of the Spirit can grow strong enough to keep all his commandments. Jesus further explained to Nicodemus,

'But whoever does what is true comes to the light' [John 3:20-21 ESV].

It is through his grace that we receive the strength to fulfil these 40 requirements and come to the light—*so an* ***entrance*** *shall be ministered unto you abundantly into the everlasting kingdom* [2 Peter 1:10-11; Matthew 6:33].

We accept all of the following rules, not just one or two of the easier ones.

To enter the Kingdom	Jesus said
John 3:5	Born of water & the spirit
Luke 13:27-28	Not be a worker of iniquity
Matthew 5:3; James 2:5	Be poor in spirit (humility)
Luke 9:62	Not look back
Matthew 5:10; Acts 14:22; 2 Thessalonians 1:4-5	Pass through persecution & tribulation
Matthew 7:20-21; Matthew 21:28-31	Do the will of the Father
Matthew 19:14; Mark 10:1; Luke 18:17	Receive the kingdom as a little child
Matthew 20:1-16	Willing to work in the vineyard
Matthew 13:8-11	Bring forth fruit
Matthew 13:47-49	Be a 'just' person
Matthew 22:2-14	Have on a wedding garment
Matthew 13:24-30; 23:13	Not be a tare or a hypocrite
Matthew 25:1-12	Have oil in their lamps
Matthew 25:14-30	Double their talents
Mark 10:23-25	Not trust in riches
	Peter said

2 Peter 1:4-11	Have Diligence, Faith, Virtue, Knowledge, Temperance, Patience, Godliness, Brotherly-Kindness and Charity abound in you.
	Paul said
1 Corinthians 6:8-10	Not be: fornicators, nor idolaters, nor adulterers, nor effeminate, nor abusers of themselves with mankind, nor thieves, nor covetous, nor drunkards, nor revilers, nor extortioners
A very similar list is found in Galatians 5:19-21, so I will include it as one concept.	Shall not commit: adultery, fornication, uncleanness, lasciviousness, idolatry, witchcraft, hatred, variance, emulations, wrath, strife, seditions, heresies, envyings, murders, drunkenness, revellings, and such like

To be Saved	**Jesus said**
Mark 16:16; John 3:22-23	Believe AND be Baptised
Luke 13:23-28	Enter through the strait gate & Not be a worker of iniquity
Luke 8:10-12; 1 Corinthians 15:1-2	Keep the word of God (*the gospel*) planted in your heart and mind
Mark 13:13; Matthew 24:13	Endure to the end

	Peter said
Acts 2:21	Call upon the name of the Lord
1 Peter 3:21	Be baptised
	Paul said
Romans 10:9-13	Confess that Jesus is Lord and God raised him from the dead
1 Timothy 2:14-15; Genesis 1:27-28	A woman will be saved through childbearing (where able) if she has faith, charity, holiness and is modest.
	King David said
Psalm 34:18	Have a broken heart and a contrite spirit

To receive Eternal Life	**Jesus said**
Luke 10:25-28	Thou shalt love the Lord thy God with all thy heart, and with all thy soul, and with all thy strength, and with all thy mind; and thy neighbour as thyself
John 12:24-26; 1 John 3:14-16	Love God more than your self
Matthew 19:16-17; John 14:21	Keep the commandments
John 4:34-36	Sow the Gospel in others hearts
John 3:16+35-36; John 6:47	Believe all he taught
John 4:14	Drink from his living waters
John 6:26-28	Labour to do the works of God
John 6:54	Eat his flesh and drink his blood
John 10:27-28	Follow him like a sheep

Revelation 21:6-7; 2:7	Overcome the world
Matthew 25:31-46	Be the kind of person who would feed the hungry, give drink to the thirsty, take the stranger in, clothe the naked, visit the sick and minister to those in prison.
	Paul said
Romans 6:19-23	Be a servant of God Servants of righteousness Have fruit of holiness (sanctification)
1 Timothy 6:10-12+18-19	Do not love money. Follow after righteousness, godliness, faith, love, patience, meekness. Fight the good fight of faith. Be rich in good works
Romans 2:6-8	Be patient in well doing & obey truth

Note: *Paul's list of entry requirements to the Kingdom given in* 1 Corinthians. 6:9-10 *was in response to questions about church members who confessed Jesus' name but have turned away from the commandments. They will not now inherit the kingdom if they do not change their ways* (i.e. 1 Corinthians. 6:8-10 *was the result of 1 Corinthians 5:11-13*).

One could summarise the above tables by saying we are saved through faith, repentance, baptism and enduring to the end in the way of Jesus Christ.

If you think the way is too hard, then you echo the exasperation of the early apostles,

‘*And they were astonished out of measure, saying among themselves, Who then can be saved?*’ [Mark 10:26]

But Jesus comforted them by saying,

‘*With men it is impossible, but not with God: for with God all things are possible.*’ [Mark 10:27]

If we join with God rather than trying to do this on our own, it is certainly possible.

I echo the words of Paul and give you my blessing and exhortation,

‘*As ye know how we exhorted and comforted and charged every one of you, as a father doth his children, that ye would walk worthy of God, who hath called you unto his kingdom and glory*’ [1 Thessalonians 2: 11-12; Matthew 22:14]

It is Real!

The kingdom of God will have galaxies, solar systems and planets associated within its dominion of thrones, principalities & powers [Revelation 21:1]. We will be made rulers over many things within. One of the holy cities that make up the kingdom might be the one we call ‘New Jerusalem’ in the book of Revelation. It will come down from heaven and be open all day, every day, for those who dwell in God’s presence. However, they must meet the requirements given above to be able to pass through the gates.

'*Blessed are they that do his commandments, that they may have right to the tree of life, and may enter in through the gates into the city.*' [Revelation 22:14;19:8]

Given the many symbolic references in scripture, it's important to remember that the kingdom of God is as real as it gets, with its own eternal law, judgment, and throne. I am so excited to consider that one day, when we are back in the presence of the Father, we will be free to look around our home and explore the kingdom!

'*He that overcometh shall inherit all things; and I will be his God, and he shall be my son.*' [Revelation 21:7]

Ten Camels

When Abraham's servant (Eliezer) went to find a wife for his master's son Isaac, he brought ten camels as a gift. The servant was a righteous man with a cunning plan. He prayed and asked the following:

'*Behold, I stand here by the well of water; and the daughters of the men of the city come out to draw water: And let it come to pass, that the damsel to whom I shall say, Let down thy pitcher, I pray thee, that I may drink; and she shall say, Drink, and I will give thy camels drink also: let the same be she that thou hast appointed for thy servant Isaac*' [Genesis 24:12-14].

Rebecca approached the well where the camels were resting, and the servant asked her for a drink,

'*And when she had done giving him drink, she said, I will draw water for thy camels also, until they have done drinking. And she hasted, and emptied her pitcher into the trough, and ran again unto the well to draw water, and drew for all his camels.*'

She brought water for all ten until they had finished drinking, which would have kept Rebecca busy for a long time, yet it is written that she quickly went to work and did not act as a slothful servant. Eliezer looked on while Rebecca served and knew the Lord had answered his prayer.

Perhaps Ruth and Rebecca both inspired Proverbs 31:10.

'*Who can find a virtuous woman? for her price is far above rubies.*'

This act was a blend of virtue, brotherly kindness and diligence.

Christ is the bridegroom (Isaac). His Father (Abraham) is the one who gave Rebecca (us) the ten camels (attributes), which we must water and nourish to demonstrate our faithfulness. Christ will know we are his on the last day, in the same way the servant knew Rebecca was to become the bride. We must hasten to the work as Rebecca did, seeking out living water and giving life to our ten camels (spiritual attributes) through quiet acts of service. She epitomised the parable of the sheep and the goats, as she knew not whom she was serving and the great blessing which awaited her [Matthew 25:32-46].

Rebecca thought she was helping a fellow servant, but in doing so, she became a joint heir of the whole world through the promises made to Abraham and Isaac [Romans 4:13].

I pray you and I will diligently nourish the ten attributes of Christ within us with the living water of the Messiah [John 4:14+25-26].

Background to the Last Entry

No life grew in Eden until the mists of living water sprang up [Genesis 2:5-6]. When Adam was cut off from the living water, he eventually died. Jesus may have addressed this when he spoke to the Samaritan woman at the well,

'*But whosoever drinketh of the water that I shall give him shall never thirst; but the water that I shall give him shall be in him a well of water springing up into everlasting life.*' [John 4:14]

The symbolism of the woman at the well with Christ and Rebecca at the well is interesting. We are encouraged to drink from the waters of life, nurturing the seed within our hearts with faithfulness—a concept that is hopefully saturated throughout Parts I and II.

Blessed and happy (*ashar* 835) are those who drink of these waters, for they shall become as a tree of life bringing forth fruit unto eternal life [Proverbs 11:30]

'*Blessed is the man ... And he shall be like a tree planted by the rivers of water, that bringeth forth his fruit in his season; his leaf also shall not wither; and whatsoever he doeth shall prosper.*' [Psalm 1:1+3]

While driving home from Norwich after writing Part II, my podcast ended. Rather than putting on music, I chose to drive in silence. In the silence, the water distilled, and the little olive tree started to grow [Psalm 1:2; 1 Kings 19:12].

The Little Olive Tree

Outside the Garden of Eden stood a young olive tree which brought forth wild fruit. He grew up with a measure of happiness as he looked around his grove of family and friends. He could see north, east and south for miles and enjoyed the beautiful vistas. Back west, a light came from the garden, obscuring his view of what was inside. The young tree would see the gardener pass between Eden and the grove each day, and they exchanged smiles now and then.

As the tree grew, he started to comprehend the light in the west garden [John 1:5] and beheld a tree in the midst of it, which bore exquisite fruit. The little olive tree was struck with wonder and began to hope that one day he could grow to be like it. Summing up courage, he asked the gardener about the tree. He answered that the tree was beautiful because of the river it lived next to. The unique waters gave life and strength to the tree. '*Please, can you dig me up and place me next to that glorious tree that I may drink of its waters also?*' asked the little olive, but the gardener said his roots were not deep enough to live there. '*Then please, can you bring me the water that I may gently nourish my roots and become stronger?*' The gardener smiled and replied that he would bring the water each time the little tree asked, but he must ask daily. The tree agreed.

As the seasons went by, the little olive grew and waxed stronger. Some of his branches brought forth good fruit as his leaves grew greener and bolder, yet others would yield wild fruit, which degraded the soil when they fell at his roots. As the gardener passed by each day, the olive tree conversed with him and asked if he could remove the bitter fruit from the ground where it fell. He expressed gratitude for the water and the change that had come upon him but one day asked why some of his fruit remained wild.

The gardener looked lovingly upon the tree and said that some of his branches would need to be removed, which would be painful. Still, if he trusted the gardener, he would replace those branches with young and tender ones from the tree in the garden. The olive was excited but scared. '*Could you just put the fruit of the tree onto my branches so I look beautiful?*' he asked. The gardener sighed as he explained that the fruit could not be grafted onto another tree, only the branches. His wild limbs would need to be removed, and new branches grafted in their place to grow fruit of their own.

Bravely, the tree agreed and watched the gardener retrieve a young and tender branch. When he returned, he was reminded that grafting was not easy, but if successful, the hard graft would be worth it over time. The young tree nodded in the wind and allowed the gardener to continue.

As the seasons rolled on, he turned over new leaves to see the fruit below. Joy filled the soil of the beaming tree as he knew the graft was working. Other trees in the grove began to take note and started to speak with the gardener.

One day, while conversing with a servant, the olive tree expressed gratitude for the change that had taken place but noted he had other branches that still yielded wild fruit, even though he was nourished daily. The servant said that more grafting would be needed over the seasons to replace the wild branches, and his soil would need to be regularly turned over and dunged about to eliminate the rotten wild fruit that had fallen.

Over time, the olive tree accepted the hard grafts and received the dung, rejoicing in the nourishing of its roots. Soon afterwards, the tree could see he was producing delicious and pure fruit from all nine branches and wondered if he was now strong enough to be taken and planted westward. He stopped the gardener and asked once more to be taken to the tree next to the stream. The gardener looked over the olive and saw the grafts were strong, as the olive tree turned over many leaves to show the fruit below. He gave the tree a smile and was pleased to see his strength but did not agree to pluck him up. '*You have all nine branches yielding delicious fruit, but your core has not finished growing*'. He explained that his trunk needed more time to receive the grafts as its own so it could produce new branches spontaneously, just as the tree in the garden does.

Over the next few seasons, the tree focused on allowing the grafts to sink deeper and deeper through its core, down to its roots. Before he could realise what was happening, new and tender branches began to shoot forth and produce fruit of their own. The little olive tree had become beautiful and fruitful, filling its soul with overwhelming joy! It now stood glorious in the grove as it lovingly watched the other olive trees, with their grafts being welded in.

The gardener passed by and stopped to speak with the tree, '*You have become beautiful, with new branches shooting forth from within you. Your roots are deep and can certainly take the flow of the stream in the garden*'. As though in the twinkling of an eye, the tree was planted next to the flowing water and stood by the side of the paradise tree. Shortly, he began issuing forth twelve new fruit, more glorious than ever, and he knew the fruit was delicious!

Now, many olive trees were looking to the garden, well on their way to allowing the strength of their grafts to sink deep into their core and produce new branches of their own.

The little olive happily stood on the right-hand side of the tree he looked up to, receiving his fullness. Now, he was always able to drink from the living waters. As the fruit fell and nourished the soil of his soul, he beamed with light. Joined by family and friends, their roots intertwined, they lived after the manner of happiness, from one eternity to the next [Ephesians 3:14-21; Malachi 4:6].

Blessed is the man who trusts in the LORD,

whose trust is the LORD.

He is like a tree planted by water,

that sends out its roots by the stream,

and does not fear when heat comes,

for its leaves remain green,

and is not anxious in the year of drought,

for it does not cease to bear fruit.

[Jeremiah 17:7-8]

'And he said unto me, It is done. I am Alpha and Omega, the beginning and the end. I will give unto him that is athirst of the fountain of the water of life freely.'

[Revelation 21:6]

Further insights from the author can be found in his book *Distant Venom*, which is scheduled for release in 2026. While it will be accessible as a stand-alone work, the author considers it to be Part III of *Grace for Grace*.

Distant Venom will answer questions about whether water baptism is necessary, how to be a light to the world, what stones John the Baptist was referring to, and many other faith-promoting thoughts gained from thirty years of writing journals as a Christian.

In the meantime, please visit *clivetwain.com* or come back to this book in about a month. Feel free to share it with a friend and discuss the contents over a hot chocolate and a cookie or two, or three, or four, or five.

Printed in Great Britain
by Amazon

60622093R00157